AF436660

Jhilmil Breckenridge is a poet, writer and activist. She is the founder of Bhor Foundation, an Indian charity, which is active in mental health advocacy, the trauma-informed approach, and providing information on other choices to heal apart from or in addition to the biomedical model. She advocates Poetry as Therapy and is working on a few initiatives, both in the UK and India, taking this into prisons and mental health institutions.

Her debut poetry collection, *Reclamation Song*, was published in May 2018 by Red River Press in India and in November 2019 by Verve Poetry Press, UK. She has co-edited a collection of essays on mental health which was published as *Side Effects of Living* (Women Unlimited and Speaking Tiger, 2019). She tweets at jhilmilspirit.

Jhilmil lives in New Delhi with her daughter, Tara, and is working on her memoir as well as a second collection of poems.

FEASTING, HEALING

Reclaiming Your Life Through Cooking

Personal Narratives, Fiction, Poetry, Recipes

Edited by

JHILMIL BRECKENRIDGE

SPEAKING
TIGER

SPEAKING TIGER BOOKS LLP
125A, Ground Floor, Shahpur Jat, near Asiad Village,
New Delhi 110049

First published by Speaking Tiger Books 2023

Anthology copyright © Speaking Tiger Books 2023
The copyright for individual essays, poems and stories
vests in the respective authors

Saima Afreen's essay, *A Portrait of Beetroot Soup*,
was published in the Bellevue Literary Review, 2022,
in a slightly different version titled *Beetroot Soup*.

ISBN: 978-93-5447-676-1
eISBN: 978-93-5447-674-7

10 9 8 7 6 5 4 3 2 1

All rights reserved.
No part of this publication may be reproduced, transmitted, or stored
in a retrieval system, in any form or by any means, electronic,
mechanical, photocopying, recording or otherwise,
without the prior permission of the publisher.

This book is sold subject to the condition that it shall not, by way of
trade or otherwise, be lent, resold, hired out, or otherwise circulated,
without the publisher's prior consent, in any form of binding
or cover other than that in which it is published.

FOR MY SON, ETHAN, WHO COOKS WITH ME

This book is also for all the broken people everywhere
who have found their way through cooking,
and for all those who still believe.

Come, eat with us.

Love after Love

Derek Walcott

The time will come
when, with elation,
you will greet yourself arriving
at your own door, in your own mirror,
and each will smile at the other's welcome,

and say, sit here. Eat.
You will love again the stranger who was your self.
Give wine. Give bread. Give back your heart
to itself, to the stranger who has loved you

all your life, whom you ignored
for another, who knows you by heart.
Take down the love letters from the bookshelf,

the photographs, the desperate notes,
peel your own image from the mirror.
Sit. Feast on your life.

CONTENTS

Preface

One night, a few years ago, sitting in Preston, UK, where I was spending a few years doing a Ph.D, I was chatting on Facebook Messenger with a friend. Both of us are foodies, have lived experiences of mental health distress and have used cooking as a means of finding ourselves. He has now become a chef and wine sommelier. I said, Mícheál, shouldn't we put together a book of our stories and others like us, add some recipes? And that is really how this book took shape!

This book is also written in part because of the huge response I got from the disabled community, from people living with mental health distress or some other psychosocial disability. These people are my tribe and I reached out in this space first. Stories started pouring in as people nodded their heads to my call for submissions. Though the book grew and there are now people who don't identify with any disability, I have to tip my hat to these first people who sent me their essays and poems.

I have to mention my friend Nusrat Durrani, whose beautiful story, *The Honeymoon*, made my editing decision suddenly expand. So far, the book was made up of personal narratives and non-fiction pieces. His piece stunned me with its poetic and brutal vision. But it was a short story! And I couldn't turn it away. I expanded the call to include a few short stories and the book kept evolving. From a melancholy essay on grief and beetroot soup to a story about Hungarian bread with a twist in the tail, I'll let you discover as you read…The book was becoming global—and the thread that ran through it was pain, followed by reclamation with food.

The book took years to curate, and suddenly we were stuck in a Covid world where people who may never have had to self-isolate or stay in, like many of my disabled friends, were doing just that. People took to cooking as they stayed home, first because of the lockdowns and later hoping to stay safe from the virus which was walking the streets, laughing and infecting countries and continents with abandon. The internet was aflood with people sharing photos and recipes for their banana bread; sourdough suddenly seemed to have caught everyone's fancy, and people were becoming more and more adventurous with their explorations in the kitchen.

There is an interest and growth in creative activities like art, writing, drumming, painting and others as a means towards resilience and recovery. Research and evidence shows that such therapies—though I always hesitate with using the term 'therapy'—indeed help with long-term trauma and healing, or in simply coping with any marginalising condition.

While accessing art or an activity like that may take time and effort, everyone needs to eat to survive and everyone has access to a kitchen. Cooking as coping is an activity with low entry barriers and in this anthology, you will find people living with disabilities, mental health conditions, angry young Pakistani women revolting against patriarchy, and more. All of them have found their way through various stressful conditions with the help of cooking or baking. As the book 'cooked', I also found people wanting to write fiction inspired by stories of cooking as reclamation and these too have found their way into the book.

In my own case, baking helped me through an abusive marriage. In 2008 I started a desserts business from home, optimistically calling it Karma Pies. The abuse and trauma definitely lead to temporary mental health distress and I remember often waking up at 3 a.m., my mind muddled with worries or thoughts of what the future may hold. What always helped was simply walking into the kitchen, making a list of the orders for the day, and by the time my family was up, cakes and pies were ready, my mind was calmer and clearer, and heavenly aromas wafted through the house! At the time, I did not consciously bake as therapy, but now know that it was the one time when my mind was calmer and I was in control as I measured, tasted, decorated and experimented. Although I am now happily divorced, I still use cooking as a means of grounding, of coming back to the here and now, and that is always a good thing.

The movement towards slow food, creating food from scratch, eschewing packaging, preservatives and the time lag from factory to table, will also help distract from tablets and smartphones, considered disastrous for people dealing with mental health issues. Slow food is more nutritious, tastes better and often has an element of sociability about it that may help mental health distress and other marginalising conditions. And not to mention, it is better for the environment and our own bellies!

So go on, get your hands to knead and chop and measure and stir. Put on that gingham apron, and show your body and your friends some love! Your own mind and body will definitely thank you.

Jhilmil Breckenridge
New Delhi, 2023

PERSONAL NARRATIVES

Cooking During the Lockdown

Manjari Agarwala

A couple of years ago, every other day was dampened by a plethora of extraneous agents. My closest relationship was arduous, my most loved one was falling sick often, I was lost regarding an identity in my career, and my dreams which I always had aplenty, were fading. I idled away the few and far between good days wishing these situations away. I promised to be disciplined, and committed, and productive, and all round exemplary, to myself and the higher powers I prayed to, if and only if, a divine intervention would liberate me from my woes.

With the passage of time, these circumstances did change. The frequency of external handicaps gradually reduced and the unencumbered good days, which used to be widely scattered, grew to become the quotidian. It took a long time to get accustomed to this new format of life, and even longer to really believe in my new reality. In my state of oscillating belief-disbelief, I was numbed into inaction. I became a champion of doing nothing. I would sit on my couch and look out on the balcony. I would stare into the withering leaves of mogra, the tissue paper like bougainvillea petals, the variegated large leaves of my monstera, the neighbouring knotted bamboo stems and out into the sky and into nothingness. Sometimes my days felt so empty, I missed the distractions of before that at least kept me going due to the rush of fight or flight. I missed being engrossed in something, anything or having an all-consuming purpose.

It wasn't that I didn't have things to do. Every other day, I would draw up an impressive to-do list—write on my blog, meet that ex-colleague, organise wardrobes and cabinets, learn to cook well and so forth—and every other day I would disappoint myself. Only essential everyday chores got done. The rest slipped into a limbo of lost dreams.

I have since resurrected myself to some degree. In the past years, I looked well and hard at my patterns and managed to free myself from some of the self-sabotaging behaviour. Yet the old ways are always waiting. In our game of hide and seek, as I get better, they often devise startling ways to find and tag me.

Sometimes it is triggered by the unavailability of a friend when I call enthused, sometimes by my mother not responding to my shower of affection in a way I'd prefer, sometimes by the aloofness of my spouse and sometimes by the information overload from the many social media apps on my phone; different things on different days. Some days, when my house help calls in sick, I get so distracted with worrying over the workings of the day that I am rendered dysfunctional. I drag my feet around the house, dressed in nightclothes, and by late afternoon, I have neither eaten nor got any chores done. I know that these seemingly tiny happenings are inevitable and I ought to be inured to them. But I'm not.

Recently, due to the corona virus outbreak and the quarantine that followed, I have been homebound and inundated with housework. In the absence of my house help and the tasks that needed doing, the sequential doorbells for newspaper, milk or ironed clothes from the dhobi that had to be answered, with little to nil engagement with regular work, I missed the regular spools around which I wound my otherwise unbridled, spilling time. With nowhere to go, yet so much to do, I was overwhelmed and full of extravagant, woolly musings. In just the first few days, I fell out of my daily yoga practice, macrobiotic diet, journal writing—all the pillars that had supported my restoration in the first place. The ensuing haze was all too familiar and I felt myself sinking again.

I knew I had to halt this spiral. I couldn't be a jingle-jangle of nerves when such a novel opportunity—to review, rethink and redesign life—presented itself. And so I began with the basics: food. I made my meals and mealtimes sacred. Brunch and dinner became my dawn and dusk—the new pegs around which everything else found space, structure and meaning.

The most so-called lacklustre culinary tasks—draining the water from soaked grains and pulses, my hands sifting through them washing them clean in spurts of running water; scrubbing the grime off potatoes and other root vegetables; peeling the skins of not so fresh, wrinkly and bendy carrots and radishes—all these activities were grounding and gratifying. These ostensibly mindless activities required my full attention and taught me lessons in mindfulness.

The cadenced movement of my new and sharp ceramic knife—neatly cutting through raw onions, carrots, bell peppers, celery stalk and zucchini—the sound of the wooden cutting board and the accompanying *khutch khutch khutch* gave me cathartic satisfaction, and the resulting vivid grid of colours before me lifted my spirit.

The *schluck schluck* of the bamboo ladle as I scraped congealed curry from the sides of a heavy iron wok; the pop of corn kernels hitting the lid of my cooker; the spluttering of mustard seeds; and the sizzle of cumin in hot oil, became a soothing salve as it quelled the chatter in my head.

While making a side of guacamole one day, I discovered the sensual pleasure of slicing through a perfectly ripe avocado, scooping out its flesh, mashing it, squeezing in lime juice, dipping my finger in it, licking it clean—finally creating a sublime work of art, which I could eat when finished! On another day, nostalgia washed over me when some leftover coconut chutney found its way into the middle of a pan-fried sandwich—a childhood favourite that had disappeared from my memory and dining table alike. And another day, while trying a new recipe from an old cookbook lying covered in dust, realising I lacked a vital spice mix, I found I had retrieved my lost instinct by replacing it effectively with ingredients I had at hand. Through all of these experiments, I found my own unique style—a balance between the method and the measure, and the test of the taste.

I became a chopping, dicing, simmering, stirring, tempering, blanching and blitz-blending sorceress, pouring spells of love and healing upon unsuspecting soups, curries and stews. The treasury of the kitchen—its sights, sounds, smells, textures and tastes—imbued my senses, uplifting them instantly, drawing me in and centering me to the present moment. They allowed me no further flights of fantasy into the void. The magic arrived and I was just present, in the here and the now.

RECIPE: MULLIGATAWNY SOUP

Ingredients:

1½ cup red lentils (masoor dhuli)
1½ tsp cold pressed coconut oil or sesame oil
I medium carrot, cut roughly
1½ cup sweet potato, cubed
1 cup pumpkin, cubed
2 onions, cut fine
1 clove
1 large bay leaf
1 or 2 cinnamon sticks
1 tsp ground cumin
1 tsp ground coriander
A pinch of cardamom powder (optional)
¼ tsp ground turmeric
4 green chillies, de-seeded and cut fine
2 or 3 whole black peppercorns or crushed black pepper
    to taste
1½ cup coconut milk, or to taste
3 to 4 cloves garlic, crushed
3 tomatoes, cut roughly
Chilli flakes, fried garlic as garnish (optional)
Spring onions, cut fine for garnishing
Salt to taste

Method:

- In a pressure cooker, sauté the onions in the oil with a pinch of salt. Add the garlic and vegetables one by one and continue sautéing.
- Add the lentils and a little water (less than a cup) and all the seasoning.

- Bring to a pressure and then simmer for 20 minutes. Or cook in a saucepan with a lid for longer, on low heat after it comes to a boil.
- Cool, remove the bay leaf, cinnamon sticks, clove.
- Blend until smooth.
- Bring back to the pot and add coconut milk.
- Garnish and serve hot.

A Portrait of Beetroot Soup

Saima Afreen

Hyderabad. The 4 p.m. winter light lit up the window. A pale rectangle fell on V's burning face. The water from the towel I wiped his forehead with swept the fever for a few more minutes before returning to claim his body, the 104°F summer refusing to leave. His lips would part now and then for a faint murmur. The paracetamol was slowly working.

His poet friend, flipping through a Holub collection, told me that he'd not eaten anything since he went into this stupor. The doctor wouldn't be here before 6 p.m. And he needed to eat something fresh, something nourishing. He convulsed. The tweed-like grey upholstery of the couch held his sleeping body above which the frame holding a yellowing poster of La Cupola di Brunelleschi stood guard almost merging into the butter-white walls. The mountainous 1436 architectural wonder in Florence looked suddenly alive in its skeletal sketch. The red of the dome was dimmer than the onion I was peeling in the kitchen.

'Everything in the mind is attached to one another like layers in an onion...' I silence the sentence of an encrgy-healer with a fresh cut, and the sliced beetroots leave maroonish-pink trails on the china bowl. Rang-e-uroos they call it—the colour of brides. Dad loved chuqandar ka halwa or uroosa halwa, as he loved to call the beetroot halwa, for its colour. His slate-grey eyes would light up from behind the newspaper seeing the sweet delight on the tea table. A few years later, the glint turned asphalt, fixed only on the lacy trim of the tablecloth fluttering in the wind. I'd close the window, draw the curtains and switch on the light, the yellow bulb a mellow sunrise above his bed. The wrinkles on his face were deep furrows filled with years of uncertain train schedules, a forsaken haveli, the Marxist flags, diaries filled with a young boy's cursives, memories of a cherry-red tie, an orchestra in the Oberoi Grand, the river Hooghly dotted with boats, a lavender sky dawning on the New Empire cinema hall. It was all naqsh (inscription) on stone. The pages in his notebook had couplets in Persian, the swollen letters silently following the trajectory of his blood for years. The world was a wounded fruit bleeding at the tip of his fountain pen, there was too much ink to write 'the end'…

The doctors had recommended thin borscht with bread cubes slightly tossed in butter for his dinner. Carrots would add a sunflower-ish tint to the beetroot soup, bright in the bowl with curled onion ringlets sleeping at the bottom. Anemones in the seabed. Unseen. Assyrian tablets mention that in 800 BCE the red vegetable grew in the Hanging Gardens of Babylon. In 300 BCE, Greeks would offer it at the temple of Delphi to Apollo. Romans ate it to heal fever.

V's forehead was hot; the burning had reduced. He still hadn't opened his eyes…His blue microfiber pullover had patches of sweat. Three cushions supported his back as he sat up and took a few spoonfuls. The lamp in the corner cast a sandalwood light. The soup was a river at night, its warmth gushing ahead. Like life. A river of chaos pushing its way forward through the throat carrying myths, songs, salt, sand, and snow.

'The sea rises, the light fails'*. A January afternoon had Calcutta wear an ashen look. There was a power cut. I stirred the soup in the candlelight; there was beauty in the red broth. Beauty I created in a simmering pot, a thin layer of olive oil deconstructing its own gleam. A dark pool which rises every night, its mouth swallowing the pit in my belly; the pen falls, the light fails…But the fingers rise with the sleeping seagrass. My face holding an ocean above dissolves in the seabed. I don't feel the weight of the millions of gallons; I feel it becoming me. Liquid silk wavering in slow motion; I can feel the atoms whirling in clusters, each drop passing through my blood. And everything becomes calm. Hours are kind strangers pushing my body in the wagon of changing landscapes.

The sun rises in another sky, its blue still brushing my father's empty bed. The notebook on the side table seems to have grown from its sheesham wood like a mushroom in the monsoon. My fingers feel blank, words fail…Several alephs together; they are tools that create, that construct. And absentmindedly I try to write, the ink fails at the curvature of the first letter. But I decide to create. Create the way each heartbeat creates blood—each drop creates more life for cells, each cell a construct of 'the now', a transmitter to the entire system. An Atlantis in the making. It always is in the making, we just choose to ignore the magic that we carry, that we are. Bruce Lipton's sermon on blood makes my fingers move. Each word is a tiny orchestra waiting for its music at fingertips. Here I was holding a knife to

---

*From James Baldwin's poem *For Nothing Is Fixed.*

create. Create something soothing that puts the tired flesh to sleep. Gently, lullaby-like. A candle left to last the night. A want to want the evening to begin with 'Once upon a time' stories told by grandma sitting on her mahogany bed or our housekeeper Chanda Bibi lighting the fire to make rotis. Her candyfloss hair lit up against the burning coals. She'd talk about djinns—creatures made of fire, her encounter with witches in the guava orchard post sunset. Or did she say midnight? Memory changes each time we linger a little longer in the past. Nothing lasts. 'We are also what we have lost'*.

The deep pink stripes in the beetroot look serpentine, a print seen through an Android filter, one among Caravaggio's decadent-luscious vegetables—symbols of desire and death. The knife carves its own itinerary through the maroon flesh.

I stir the simmering cerise broth. The low flame pushes the slices of beetroot, carrots and tomatoes into a slow dance swirling to the centre. Bubbling in the pot. A candlelight sonata I cannot hear. The sea is rising again... It fills my mouth, my eyes, my hair, the tip of my toes, the walls in my heart; waves crash against my bones. What's broken doesn't break; it just dissolves with water, becoming memory. There's chaos and then peace. And slowly it all quietens down. The sea still roars, but something within me connects with the enormity of grief. I surrender, allowing it to take over my mind and body. To un-construct each cell, each beat, each drop till I pulsate with grief almost like a wind-eaten temple which smells of hymns and sins alike. To feel with such intensity is also to dive deep into my consciousness, to turn the un-constructed parts upside

---

*Lines from the movie *Amores Perros*

down and see what remains unwoven outside of it. To surrender again. To feel grief as grief is. To understand that grief is also me...

I pour more soup for V. He says he feels better. I begin folding his white pashmina. The mountain of my palm still stained with the pink juice, in the same spot when I'd prepared it the last time for myself at Canterbury in the spring of 2019, before leaving for Stirling, keeping a portion on the breakfast table for Benedikt, my housemate, whose ruddy face was redder because of a persistent cold he had caught in Frankfurt. In the LNER train coach, sitting opposite to me, is Olga, a virologist from Romania, who talks about her research on harp-like movement in blood cells when they transfer food. I smile and she spots the stain on my palm. It wouldn't go even when I rubbed it with an aloe vera wipe. Stubborn in its stay. Demanding surrender again. In its impudence I find peace. In its bleeding, beauty.

Recipe: Beetroot Soup

Ingredients:

1 large beetroot—washed, peeled and sliced
2 carrots—washed, peeled and halved
2 tomatoes—washed, halved
1 onion—washed, peeled and sliced
¼ inch ginger—washed, peeled and halved
1 or 2 tsp coriander leaves—washed and finely chopped
One large tbsp olive oil
One clove
Salt to taste
A pinch of pepper powder
Three cups of water

Method:

- Heat oil in a pressure cooker, add the clove and let it crackle.
- Add all the chopped vegetables and sauté for a minute.
- Add salt, pepper powder and coriander leaves followed by water.
- Put the lid and let it cook for six whistles on medium flame or till the vegetables are done.
- Remove from heat.
- Segregate the vegetable chunks from the broth.
- Serve the soup hot with a blob of butter.

A Foodie in a Foreign Land

Kathakoli Dasgupta

Given my relationship with food today, it's hard to imagine that I used to be a fussy eater.

I can't remember if the love was gradual. What I do recall is that after having lost a lot of weight after a bout of illness during my final year at college, my gran, Moni, vowed to send me back home to Delhi three kilos heavier after a month at hers (in Kolkata). The plan involved three home-cooked wholesome meals plus lots of snacks throughout the day.

I still remember looking forward to the rui maachh bhaja (rohu/carp fish fried in mustard oil) and aloo bhaja (fried matchstick potatoes) with masoor daal and bhaat (boiled rice) I had for breakfast most mornings. Until then I used to loathe rui maachh. B-o-r-i-n-g! But there was something appetising about the pungent whiff of hot mustard oil mixed with the smell of fresh river fish, combined with the sneeze-triggering tempering of green chilli and radhuni in the dal that made my mouth water and beckoned me to the dinner table.

I also started to spend more time with Moni in the kitchen watching her prepare the daily five-course lunch and dinner meticulously, helping her sometimes.

There was a certain rhythm, dare I say, music, in all the cutting, scraping and grinding. I loved how her hands moved dexterously on the razor sharp bonti as she diced vegetables—all the same size—for shukto or chorchori. I was fascinated by the rocking motion of her slender wrists on the old narkel kuruni and the heirloom shil nora that she used to make bata (pastes) of shorshe (mustard seed), posto (white poppy seed) or even masala, to enhance the flavour and consistency of any jhol (a runny curry). I studied her as she intuitively matched the tempering spice to the dish—kalo jeere for lau chingri, shada jeere for aloo phoolkopi, paanch phoron for chorchori, and so on. A pinch of this, a dash of that, never too much, never too little.

I think it was probably in that old, dark, hot and greasy kitchen that I 'discovered' food and the joys of cooking and unknowingly fell in love with it.

This relationship, which continues to grow, has served me well over the years. I have relied on the therapeutic benefits of cooking to see me through stressful days or challenging times. More than anything else, I love the emotions a good plate of food brings out.

For one, I am convinced that it brings people together. I have made so many friends over a cake or a curry. I have connected with complete strangers in countries I have visited over a local ingredient or dish. A few years back in Greece, finding similarities between some Indian and Greek foods, the chef and I got talking around the Ottoman influence on Greek cuisine as well as the spice trade via the silk route that would have made the similarities possible. Fascinating!

I have felt humbled seeing how a bowl of home-cooked daal and vegetables helped to trigger the taste buds of our neighbour who had lost her appetite due to chemotherapy. Or more recently, how some packed dinner livened up the spirits of a family coping with cancer diagnosis of a near one. I felt overjoyed when my 91-year-old English father-in-law (now, deceased) remarked after a Bengali feast that he had tried new foods since I had come into the family and relished them all. I feel rewarded seeing guests enjoy every bite I have put my heart and soul into. And nothing is more satisfying than when my husband, Dave, and I sit down for a home-cooked meal after a hard day and find our stresses melt away with every spoonful.

Food has helped me deal with the challenges I met with after I moved to the UK with my husband a few years ago. I struggled to find a job, I felt lonely and homesick. I turned to food again and found infinite happiness in cooking and feeding. I also used the time I now had to hone my culinary skills.

Far from feeling constrained by the lack of availability of some staples in my larder back in India, I felt challenged and enthused to use the locally available ingredients to make foods that reminded me of home. It also forced me to adopt traditional ways of doing things. I started making more and more ingredients, from paneer to regional spice mixes, from scratch. The difference in the taste and texture of food is noticeable.

The move has allowed me to try many exotic ingredients. I absolutely love going down the aisles in the supermarkets here, scanning the huge array of foods from different parts of the world. I pick up a jar of this and a bottle of that and then experiment. Similarly, I derive huge and constant inspiration from our little herb garden and fresh produce that friends bring me from theirs.

It has also led me to experiment with different methods of cooking. The iconic TV programme, the Great British Bake Off, for example, has led me to take on baking. I always thought I was far too roguish to be a good baker, as baking requires scientific precision. But I have surprised myself! Would I be boasting if I added that a few years ago I received the trophy in the confectionary category at our village horticultural show?

As my confidence soared in the new world, I decided to take the plunge and fulfil my dream of starting my own food venture in September 2019. So here I am running a catering business that is growing at a comfortable pace, despite the challenges that Covid brought on. In fact, I used it as an opportunity to reimagine, reshape and diversify my business and service. Though in doing so I never lost sight of the core values that define my business—of showcasing the diverse cuisine and culture of India, offering people foods that tell a story, giving them a taste of everything I have picked up over the years, everything I learn daily. A sum total, with infinite possibilities.

RECIPE: RASPBERRY CARDAMOM WHITE CHOCOLATE CUPCAKES

Makes 24 mini cupcakes

For the cupcakes:

100 gm unsalted butter, softened, at room temperature
85 gm golden castor sugar
2 large eggs
100 gm self-raising flour, sifted with salt
A pinch of salt
3 tbsp milk

½ tsp cardamom powder
1½ tbsp freeze-dried raspberries (plus extra for
   sprinkling)
Mini cupcake tray
Mini cupcake liners
Hot water in an oven-safe bowl

For the icing:

200 gm cream cheese
100 gm butter, softened, at room temperature
100 gm icing sugar
A tsp of vanilla extract (optional)
For the chocolate shards:
30 gm cooking white chocolate, broken or chopped
A big pinch of cardamom powder
A tray lined with greaseproof paper

Method:

- Beat butter and sugar until, creamy and fluffy.
- Whisk in the eggs, one by one. If the batter seems to curdle, add a tsp of the sifted flour.
- Add cardamom powder and milk. Stir with a wooden or silicone spatula. Now add the sifted flour in 2 to 3 batches, gently folding. Add the freeze-dried raspberries with the last batch of flour. The batter should be of dropping consistency—if it seems too thick, add a dash of milk.
- Preheat oven to 150°C (fan assisted). Put a bowl of hot water at the bottom. This creates steam which prevents a dome in cupcakes.
- Line the mini cupcake tray with mini cupcake liners. Divide the batter between 24 cupcakes.

- Bake for 18 to 20 minutes or until a skewer inserted comes out clean.
- Let them cool in the tray for 5 minutes; then take them out on a cooling rack.
- Melt broken or chopped white chocolate in the microwave or using a double boiler. Mix in the cardamom powder.
- Line a flat tray with greaseproof paper. Spread the melted chocolate on the tray as evenly as possible. Chill in the fridge for at least two hours. Once chilled, cut into shards.
- For the icing, beat butter with icing sugar until smooth. Add the cream cheese and vanilla extract, if using, and beat again to combine. Put into a piping bag fitted with your favourite piping tip. Keep cool, until ready to use. Once the cupcakes have cooled completely, pipe the cream cheese. Sprinkle freeze-dried raspberries and insert a white chocolate shard in each.

Glossary:

Note: Most non-English words are in the Bengali

Aloo phulkopi: potato and cauliflower vegetable curry

Bonti: a traditional curved blade on a narrow wooden platform; the user stabilises the blade with one foot, holding the vegetable, fish or meat with both hands, sliding it backwards and forwards against the curving blade

Chorchori: mixed seasonal vegetables

Kalo jeere: nigella seeds

Lau chingri: a popular Bengali dish of diced bottle gourd and shrimps, usually cooked with milk

Narkel kuruni: a traditional coconut scraper, similar to the bonti but with a flat round top that has serrated edges; the shell of the coconut halves are held with both hands and the fleshy inside is scraped against the serrated edges

Paanch phoron: a tempering spice mix used predominantly in Bengali cuisine; consists of mustard, fennel, fenugreek, nigella, radhuni/cumin seeds

Radhuni: a tempering spice typically used in Bengali cuisine; similar flavour to caraway and wild celery seeds

Shada jeere: cumin seeds

Shil-nora: a flat stone version of the mortal (shil) and pestle (nora) used to make a paste with spices and ingredients like ginger, garlic and onions; the spices are put in the middle of the flat stone with a sprinkle of water, the ends of the nora are held with both hands, the grinding is done slowly in a rocking motion

Shukto: a bitter stew of vegetables that is had at the start of a Bengali meal to stimulate the appetite

Finding My Way through Anxiety
with Cooking

Mekhala Saran

A tablespoon of butter sizzles on the pan. Two broken elaichi, the cardamom tossed in for aroma. I don't know the correct way of chopping onions, so as with all things in life, I decide to wing it. Doesn't turn out half bad. I am convinced onions have seeds and everybody who has told me otherwise has lied to me. Regardless of the guilt I feel about wasting, I leave a suspicious little central piece of onion out. I don't want my friends, coming over for dinner, to accidentally eat seeds. I don't know how to peel garlic either, so my cooking is usually devoid of garlic. But my friends promise me it is not devoid of flavour. I choose to believe them.

I have never intently watched anybody cook, except in YouTube videos. I was never very interested, until I shifted to Noida and started living alone in a tiny flat in a high-rise building. Suddenly I had an entire, albeit decrepit, kitchen at my disposal, and enough supplies to experiment with. The first dish I made was khichdi, for a friend who had an upset stomach. My mom narrated the recipe on speakerphone, and clumsily, amateurishly, I threw in rice, daal and ghee and whipped up a satisfying bowlful of khichdi. As I watched my friend gobble down something I had created, I felt oddly empowered. When he told me the next morning that his stomach felt a whole lot better, I felt unreal. In cooking, I found magic. I could now soothe an upset stomach, cure a bad cold and mend an aching heart—sometimes of others, and quite often, my own.

From khichdi, I went on to make black pepper chicken, meatballs in coconut curry, noodles, soup, puddings and cake. I preferred not to stick to any recipe, throwing in spices of my choosing, inhaling the aroma, tasting a teaspoonful, adding water, adding yoghurt, adding sugar, adding ghee and seeing what I could come up with. Every time it was something new, every time it was something different. I'd found in me a superpower, it seemed. My old-fashioned kitchen became my theatre, and my performance an escape from the struggles of a mundane existence.

It took me a while, however, before I realised that cooking meant more to me than just making something for my friends to enjoy and compliment me on. For many months, I had only believed that my cooking was transactional: I fed my friends and in return they watered my narcissistic soul. Until, one evening, I had an argument with a friend and I switched off my phone, tossed it on to my bed and rushed into the kitchen. In that moment, as I stood facing the stove, a pot of water boiling and bubbling before me, I realised how easily cooking helped me switch off from all else. I think I made a thin, tangy tomato soup and a vegetable sandwich that night.

Since before I can remember, I have struggled with anxiety. As a teenager, I would tug at dead ends of my chapped fingers and once my skin was rough enough, I would rub it against any soft fabric. As I watched the fabric cling to the chapped bits sticking out of my fingertips, I felt empowered. In cooking I found a similar, a stronger and a healthier sense of empowerment. People who ate my food translated into the soft fabric, their eating became the clinging action and my cooking equated with the tugging.

At the age of twenty-four, as a young adult with endless insecurities, often pertaining to the self, I had always found respite in small experiences of success. I'd scrounged for it in all aspects of my life, and often had my heart broken. The trouble is not that mediocrity in itself is bad. There's a huge difference between being mediocre and being bad. The trouble is that the awareness of one's own mediocrity in a world full of gleaming experts and seeming winners can be an isolating experience for a beginner on the grown-up scene. It can make one question their self-worth, and question whether they are capable of doing anything at all. This is probably because everyone else looks so successful on Instagram and talks so well on Twitter.

But every time I am able to whip up a dish I feel successful. And I'm not a great cook. I have burnt food, I have spilled soup and let my groceries rot. I am in no way an expert, and some of my experiments with food, as with life, are downright ridiculous. Sometimes, however, amid all the burning and the spilling and the rotting, I find small wins, and those wins heal my soul in more ways than one.

So come over for a meal? Tonight I'm making chicken balls in a thick gravy of butter and curd, with red chilli and chaat masala for flavour, garam masala for intensity, broken elaichi for aroma and hope for the soul. No garlic, however, and no faux expertise.

Recipe: Feel-good Egg Sandwich

This is based on my aunt's egg sandwich recipe that my mother shared with me on the phone on a very warm and lazy summer evening. I tweaked it slightly to suit me better, and also because I don't enjoy following any pre-shared recipe entirely.

Ingredients:

3 eggs
4 slices of bread—cut in halves
1 small onion—chopped
2 tablespoons of melted butter
Salt
Red chilli powder—a pinch

Method:

- Boil the eggs for 3 to 5 minutes. The boiled eggs should be semi-hard.
- Let the eggs cool and then peel them.
- Mash the eggs and add melted butter, letting the butter blend into the egg yolk.
- Add chopped onions, a pinch of red chilli and salt to taste.
- Mix well, and use a spoon to spread the mixture evenly between halves of bread.
- The sandwich is best enjoyed with a glass of cold coffee.

Searching for the Perfect Chocolate Brownie through a Haze of Pain

Srinidhi Raghavan

The phone vibrated next to my head. I answered it but words never left my mouth. That was when I realised I didn't actually answer the call. That one or the many that followed. I felt like I had but it was my exhausted mind playing tricks. I sent them all apology notes, depending on how well we knew each other. 'Sorry, too tired to talk today.' 'Not feeling too well today so resting.' Versions of the same thing, modified, changed to fit the person on the other end.

It was my birthday. People were calling to wish me. The kind thing to do but I am not fond of birthdays. My partner tried to wake me up at midnight but I didn't notice. I was too fatigued and fast asleep. He didn't get worried for another twelve hours—he is used to me sleeping a lot. He gently prodded me awake around 11 a.m. 'Are you okay? I am going to work.' Was I okay? 'Yes, yes. Don't worry. I am just a bit tired today. Were you worried?'

'Just a bit,' he said, as he looked very concerned. He gave me a gentle kiss as he headed off to work.

I stayed in bed most of the day. I woke up only to make myself a meal. I made myself some noodles—gluten-free with some hard cheese that my friend had gifted me the day before, which I ate with the only TV show I can watch right now, *Gilmore Girls*.

Pasta was easy to make and didn't require me to stand in the kitchen for too long. The gluten-free pasta was meant to be a treat for myself. Just cook some vegetables, the noodles separately and add the two together. Serve with a generous topping of cheese. It is something I make with ease and it is comfort food after all. I fell back to sleep through the rest of the day, interrupted only by the doorbell delivering presents from my lovely friends and some more calls, which I missed. I couldn't get myself to speak to anyone. I apologised some more. At the end of the day, tired and upset I had done nothing special, I baked myself a cake. Baking was among the things I did to feel better. Baking meant a lot of whisking. Whisking that exhausted me. Yet, I wanted my grumpy mood to be pushed away for a bit. Plus, we all deserve cake, right? My partner and I cut it quietly and I crawled back into bed.

Cooking, despite the fatigue that ensued, was a way for me to deal with the pain and the bad moods that came along with it. The cooking helped me focus on something and that made everything a lot better. Good food at the end of the process was only an added bonus.

Pain is such a mysterious being. With constant pain came a companion, exhaustion. Medically they say depression and anxiety are comorbid symptoms for fibromyalgia and basically most chronic illnesses. The terms are throwaway language for emotional baggage, I feel, and probably many, many others who live with chronic conditions who spend so many hours of our lives in our bed, away from most people's eyes. 'Of course your mental health takes a toll, you are in pain all day,' my doctor stated.

I have lived with pain for a few years now. About a year after discovering my consistent pain, I was asked by a doctor to go on a gluten-free and lactose-free diet. Initially, it was a shocker for me. I began by taking a look at all the products I bought regularly and so many of them had gluten and lactose in it. I needed to entirely forget eating desserts outside, my absolute favourite part of any meal. Cooking, therefore, became a necessity. Home-cooked food was a good way to ensure my meals were safe and prepared without any of these ingredients.

Though I have cooked for several years now, falling ill and cooking my meals led to the discovery that cooking was part of my healing process. Cooking my meals taught me to involve myself in the process. The cutting, a careful look at every ingredient, sautéing the food, all added to the calm that filled me; it reminded me to focus on the process, the journey as much as the end result. A lesson relevant to my life itself.

Since store-bought sweets were out of the question, I went out and bought myself some baking implements and entirely gluten- and lactose-free ingredients. It was exciting and exhausting. I first began by baking cakes. They turned out sometimes too hard, sometimes not cakey enough. I baked many cakes and eventually, they got better. Most of the recipes were taken off the internet and tweaked to meet my diet. The internet was the best cookbook I could ask for, with luscious photos of gluten- and lactose-free desserts. Among these you couldn't do better than Nigella Lawson's recipe for chocolate cake, a tried and tested recipe that never failed me. Other cakes, especially fruity ones like chocolate with orange, chocolate with apricot, I looked up and the internet provided. The oat flour, the rice flour, the buckwheat flour were all tested to be made into perfect cookies and cakes. I researched and understood which flours provided the fat, which lactose-free milk was better (it is always coconut milk). Slowly and steadily, I began to make cakes for others. My neighbours and friends were only too delighted and provided feedback. This made me look for more complex recipes like Christmas cakes with no gluten or lactose which turned out to be delicious! All the exploring meant I spent more time in the kitchen. And so, more time spent on healing.

While on this diet, which lasted more than a year, I questioned if my pain had reduced. It hadn't but through this process I built a deeper relationship with the food I ate. And I added baking and cooking to my self-care regime. The knowledge that whipping together cocoa powder and hot water would result in a beautiful mixture kept me going on tough days. The process of baking was as relaxing and reassuring as the process of eating. After a while, I made more cakes than I wanted to eat. Yet, I continued baking almost religiously.

During my years of baking, one day I returned from a frustrating doctor experience. There was lots of dismissal of my pain and a lot more unanswered questions. I stormed into our tiny house and dropped all my bags. I walked straight into the kitchen and began to bake a cake. I was not a baking natural (I believed and still do that some people are). I needed recipes and followed them to a T. I looked for complex gluten- and lactose-free recipes online but I found none that excited me. So, I went rogue and baked a cake filled with rum, raisins, walnuts and almonds. It was more brownie than cake but it might have been the best one I ever made. With my mind more at ease, I went to bed that night; the house smelt of freshly baked chocolate goodness.

Ever since I started baking, I had been craving to make that perfect gluten-free brownie. The pictures and recipes on the internet were vast and vibrant so I had been drowning in ideas. Yet, somehow every one I tried had something or the other wrong with it. One week I thought I would try a blondie. To be honest, I had never eaten a non-gluten free blondie. So I had nothing to compare these with. However, my learning curve with food had taught me that I needed to understand why many of my cakes, brownies, etc., made with gluten-free flour tended to collapse.

As much as I would love to share the recipe for this blondie, I don't think I should. It fell in the middle. It was a fudgy mess, although the perfect picture I took of it looked otherwise. The corners were salvaged. The middle was frozen and eaten with a spoon. Instead, I reflected on my serious difficulties with 'failures' in the kitchen vs. the 'beautiful' photographs. The recipe world was a giant collection of beautiful, serene perfection.

I wouldn't change my journey because the process of cooking has deepened my engagement with food in so many ways. It helped me understand balance in foods better, question my tastes and preferences. In baking gluten-free, I slowly learned to move away from processed sugar. Many years ago people told me how harmful it was and somehow I never listened as I consumed buckets full of candy. Literally buckets full. It was such a pretty sight, me and my candy, together till something pulled us apart. Now I find my body rejects the sugar even before I even buy it. Similarly, recently when I ate gluten during a cheat meal, my body was not happy. I have been led to think a lot more about food, cooking, self-care and healing. Cooking and baking brought me closer to my body and helped me listen to my body's needs while creating some lovely food in the process, food I put on my own plate and the plates of those I love.

Today, I hope you have had a plate of food that your body truly enjoys.

RECIPE: DEVIL'S FOOD CAKE

Recipe inspired by Nigella's Devil's Food Cake
but happily made my own...

Ingredients:

50 gm cocoa powder
200 gm sugar
250 ml boiling water
125 gm soft unsalted butter (plus some for greasing)
225 gm all-purpose flour
½ tsp baking powder
½ tsp bicarbonate of soda
3 large eggs
Whiskey-soaked raisins and nuts

Method:

- Put the cocoa and half of the sugar into a bowl and pour in the boiling water. Whisk to mix, then set aside.
- Cream the butter and the remaining sugar together, beating well until pale and fluffy.
- Stir the flour, baking powder and bicarb together in another bowl, and set aside for a moment.
- Break an egg into the creamed butter and sugar, quickly followed by a scoopful of flour mixture, then the second egg.
- Add the whiskey-soaked raisins and nuts and mix it with a ladle.

- Keep mixing and add the rest of the dried ingredients for the cake, then finally mix and fold in the cocoa mixture.
- Butter a dish and pour the mixture into it.
- Bake at 180°C/350° F for 35—45 minutes or when the knife comes out clean.
- Serve hot or put in the fridge and eat later. Both ways will turn out great, I am sure! Enjoy!!

The Meze Table

Rebecca Vedavathy B.

The Mediterranean style meze table is a sit-down meal with a variety of appetisers served and savoured while friends and family enjoy intimate conversations created by the pleasant ambience and food (sometimes drinks are involved too). The home-cooked food and drinks that are laid out on a Mediterranean meze table are not things I am going to tell you about. I will, however, tell you about the origins of my meze table and why I, an Indian woman, needed one.

In the winter of 2017, I went to live in Montreal for five months. Montreal is a cosmopolitan city in all ways but one. Montreal loves its French uncompromisingly. There is, without doubt, a postcolonial precedent to this monopoly. Knowing this history full well, speaking in English in such a milieu did not seem like the best idea especially for someone trying to have an immersive cultural experience. So, I made sentence after sentence in French. I tried to remain curious, child-like—learn the French names of spices and everyday objects, even kitchen appliances because these aren't always the things a foreign language classroom teaches you; I wonder why. But it didn't take me long to realise, what one would learn as 'standard French' in an Indian French classroom validated by the Gods of the Hexagon was not the French spoken by the Quebecois people. Of course, like any good student of Quebec literature, we did read *Les Belles-sœurs* by Michel Tremblay and *Bonheur d'occasion* by Gabrielle Roy—not to forget the many works of immigrant writers in Quebec like Dany Laferrière and Marie-Célie Agnant. But nothing prepared me for the distinct sense of dissonance that would overwhelm me while trying to decipher the phonetics, vocabulary and syntax that guided this French that suddenly became a living being articulated outside a classroom. I could feel it in my bones. After every conversation in this language I would feel emptied out. This was after spending fifteen years of my adult life studying French. Obviously, there is no better way to break the 'standard French' myth in the mind of a French student.

The postcolonial politics of language is what drew me to French Quebec literature but also exactly what estranged me from myself when I began to live in Montreal. Suddenly the bilingual poem, *Speak What,* by Marco Micone began to make more sense. Micone, an Italian immigrant writer in Montreal, penned his poem *Speak What* in response to the poem *Speak White* by Michèle Lalonde, a Quebecois writer. *Speak White* was written in 1968 by Lalonde in an attempt to subvert the commonly used slur 'speak white' (used by English speakers in Canada at the time) which translated to 'speak English and not French in public'. French speakers in Quebec who faced linguistic marginalisation strongly related to Lalonde's iconic poem for its ability to evoke the linguistic oppression they faced. However, with the number of immigrants in Quebec rising rapidly a few decades later in 1989, Marco Micone wrote his poem *Speak What* which speaks about the marginalisation of new populations who moved to Quebec. Micone writes:

speak what
no one understands you
not at St. Henri nor at Montreal-Nord
we speak the language of silence
and of powerlessness.*

This is to say that the formerly marginalised French speakers suddenly began to impose their linguistic superiority over the new immigrant populations who felt silenced and powerless. I felt so connected to the lines 'no one understands you' because I truly was left unable to understand the most basic of things.

Imagine this: every time one of my flatmates asked me to put on my socks or zip up my pullover or cussed, they would not use the words socks or pullover or fuck (or the 'standard French' equivalent my brain was trained in). They didn't say '*des chaussettes*' or '*un pull*' or '*merde*', which are words for socks and pullovers and fuck in French. Instead they would use '*des bas*' or '*une doudoune*' or '*câlis de criss*' in a completely different accent and not always in a familiar syntax. Any illusions that I harboured about the arbitrariness of language were wiped clean from the slate of my not-so-tabula rasa mind.

At first, I politely requested people to repeat themselves. They always politely explained themselves—the way one would treat an acquaintance—out of their characteristic Canadian politeness. Not so bad at first but with time, it began to take a toll. I felt left out of conversations that were about the now and the everyday that didn't pause for

---

*https://www.google.co.in/books/edition/Pluriel/6LE-DwAAQBAJ?hl=en&gbpv=1&dq=%22speak+what%22+micone+%22il+est+si+beau%22&pg=PA84&printsec=frontcover

me or anyone else. I began to realise that I slowed down people's conversations by seeking explanations or taking too long to tell my story. Every time, my flatmates hosted a house party I was paralysed by fear about what I would say if someone didn't take the time to speak at a slower pace. I obviously had my initial few conversations down pat. My name is…I study…I am from…I enjoy…What do you do…Ah…Interesting…I enjoyed reading X…you too… That's amazing…What did you like about it…If you like this writer, you'll definitely love this one too…No, I haven't heard of her…Oh…You should definitely read her…Cool…

What do you do when you run out of the generic stuff? Then what? Imagine your mind is wiped of not just all familiar semantic moorings but also cultural references people your age religiously refer to. You don't know Arundhati Roy or Paul Taylor or *Modern Family* or the Beatles or *Schitt's Creek* or Salman Rushdie or Faye D'Souza or Danish Sait or Jacinda Ardern. Imagine every time someone said 'bevarsi kudka' or sang 'hum dekhenge' you had no idea why. These are topical references gathered only when you live a culture, not something that can be acquired in a classroom. Of course, I had read books from the Quebec canon, I had heard of one Indian-Quebecois comedian, 'Sugar Sammy', and knew a few immigrant stories. But I didn't listen to the same music; I didn't catch the words or the rhythm of the songs they played. The fairy tales, myths and carols that structured my mind were so very different from the ones they heard or sang or narrated. I felt alienated in those cold winter months, not because someone treated me badly but because I couldn't always understand what someone was trying to say and more importantly, because I never felt understood. Native French speakers from other

Francophone countries felt this way, as Micone's poem suggests. I was clearly not alone. However, this poem is a gift only hindsight can afford. I didn't think of this poem or anything else that could remotely make me feel more welcome. This was a new feeling for me. Language was always my peace offering to make 'the other' my own. I've made most of my friends with silly puns and long telephone conversations. Words have always helped me express the most nuanced of thoughts. I didn't realise until one cold Christmas Eve that not all words in all languages were willing friends who permitted me the luxury of expressing myself clearly. In this new country, in the dead of winter, in the midst of a room full of people enjoying a Christmas dinner, I had never felt more alone.

This was when I resorted to cooking. Before Montreal, not learning to cook was an act of rebellion; a trump card for when someone would not be able to introduce me to a prospective groom as a girl who knew how to cook. In defying this stereotype, I discounted the pleasures of cooking. However, in Montreal, I was much like Kulfi, from Kiran Desai's novel *Hullabaloo in the Guava Orchard*. Overnight, I developed a fondness for escaping into the kitchen and cooking meals for my flatmates, their friends, and mine. In a foreign place, much like Kulfi's outdoor kitchen, I took to not only communicating through my favourite Indian flavours with exotic ingredients but by also experimenting with new ones. I sought comfort in a warm bowl of paruppu saadam (daal and rice in Tamil) some evenings while sipping on $10 wine straight from the bottle. Some others, I watched as X and C made fish and chips or a ramen bowl. I helped them cut the vegetables, wash the dishes and they helped me decipher the names of objects that eluded me. Some days, I felt closer to home when J brought Mexican tacos to our table. He made all the little assemblages, except for the tortilla shells that he sourced from the Mexican grocer. He taught me tortillas are more like chapatis and less like the corn shells we eat at Taco Bell. Assembling the shredded beef, lettuce leaves, guacamole, salsa and pickles together on a table allowed me a feeling of communion with people. A place where I didn't have to talk; a place of doing.

The table we shared, as I learnt later on, was from a thrift shop in Montreal. The aged wooden chairs did not match the table, or each other. But, sitting on it cross-legged I learnt the easier name for potatoes, *'les patates'*, as opposed to their French cousins *'les pommes de terre'*, or *'les bluets'* for blueberries as opposed to *'les myrtilles'*. I even picked up some pretty cool expressions like cherry on the sundae, *'la cerise sur la sundae'* (killing that dreadful expression wrongly attributed to Marie Antoinette about the cake once and for all), and how some expressions like *'avoir un pain au four'* remained the same as their English counterparts 'to have a bun in the oven'.

These linguistic anchors helped me, but there continued to be moments that disconcerted me—when someone said *'dîner'* they meant lunch and *'déjeuner'* when they meant breakfast. On one occasion, I didn't turn up to a *'dîner'* I was invited to by a professor because she said the word *'dîner'* so many times I believed I was being invited to dinner and not to lunch. It caught me completely off guard when she called me at 12.30 p.m. asking me where I was that afternoon. In midday Montreal traffic, I had to hail a cab and head downtown to get to my appointment. I made it and she didn't seem angry. As she bought me one of the most expensive and tasty meals of my life with the famous French dish, *les escargots au beurre* (snails cooked in herb-butter sauce), I realised this was perhaps her language of kindness.

There were other moments when I immensely enjoyed the $5 salad from the university canteen as I wrote about the snow falling in straight lines from the slanted roof of the building. I also came to love boiled beetroots in a salad. The beets were cubed after boiling, mixed with salad leaves (roquette, lettuce of any kind), cherry tomatoes, feta cheese, walnuts, sunflower seeds and a balsamic vinegar dressing. The best part about this salad was that the water in which the beetroots were boiled could be used to water plants. I loved being the bearer of nourishment to the indoor plants in temperatures that hit as low as −40°C.

I discovered tomatoes, coconut milk and chickpeas in a can. Since most fruits and vegetables are imported into Canada from parts of South America, these were easier alternatives to fresh produce that was not always readily available. If ever I felt terribly homesick, I would take myself to the warmth of the gurudwara that served some of the simplest meals that warmed the soul. Another way I felt right at home was when I walked to China Town by myself and slurped a warm bowl of spicy soup. It was not just the soup that drew me to China Town; the waiters spoke to me in English. These little escapades made me forget my inability to always contribute to Quebecois French conversations.

Sharing meals with these new friends I had made only because of food gave me purpose at the table. They loved the food I cooked, and some made requests from my limited repertoire of Indian food. I made butter chicken for the first time, not in India but in Montreal. It speaks volumes about the cross-cultural value of butter chicken. Any Indian restaurant outside India across the globe definitely carries one or the other form of butter chicken on their menu; the signature dish that somehow seems to represent us as a culture. I can't decide if it's a good or a bad thing. I enjoyed experimenting with the butter chicken though. But most of all I enjoyed making simple chicken and prawn curries with rich canned coconut milk. Did you know that curry leaves freeze beautifully? I used them, two months after I had bought them, in my prawn coconut curry and the fragrance that wafted through the entire house transported me to a tiled-roof Kerala kitchen back home. I silently manoeuvred through these cultures via my encounters with curry leaves, thorny Nopal cactus, boiled beetroots, pink-veined prawns, homemade beef broth and warm buttered bagels. Not all of these meals could be shared, most of them were eaten alone—something that really affected me.

Many months after I came back home to India, I continued to live in the haze of having been lost to a language. Living in a hostel, I had also lost my escape in food. I ate mess food that was fresh but I found myself lost more than ever. This time, D opened his little apartment kitchen to my culinary and linguistic adventures. We exchanged very few words as we began cooking. We cooked affordable Indian food every evening for almost a year. In this kitchen, I allowed him to care for me. I no longer made elaborate dishes like butter chicken. I chopped onions as he taught me how to roll parathas evenly. Some days we walked down the street to a bhaiyya who sold homemade paneer and ghee. With these ingredients, D would create his signature melt-in-your-mouth matar (peas) pulao while he allowed me to work on my writing. Other days he would go grocery shopping by himself and buy vegetables that I didn't really enjoy along with my favourite bar of chocolate that would be laid out for me in the fridge as I opened it. Slowly, he began to cure my aversion to brinjals and peas. He even made me fall in love with his laal saag or amaranth stir-fry. He cooked the slightly tangy leaves in a combination of mustard oil, cumin seeds, green chillies, mustard seeds, coriander and turmeric powder as I stood watching. He whipped up entire meals in just half an hour including the famous Bihari tawa-fried litti-chokha (stuffed wheat dough balls and mixed vegetables) and sattu (roasted gram flour) parathas.

He would permit me my South Indian sins of eating curd (yoghurt) with brinjal fry, litti-chokha, laal saag and other odd combinations. Packets of yoghurt would show up in the fridge for me to eat along with my meals. I would also add a broken Hindi that I began to rely on to my list of sins, as a return to myself. I gendered objects as I pleased and filled in my lack of a real Hindi vocabulary with many an English word.

In my hope to recreate my prawn curry from Montreal, I once ordered frozen prawns. The prawns stunk up the entire kitchen and gave us both a bad tummy. He didn't make a big fuss about it. The only thing he would ask me once in a while was to make dosas. He cooked his chicken in only a gravy of onions unlike my elaborate curries. He made the tastiest food with the simplest of ingredients. He didn't force me to explain my silences. Since neither of us liked to wash dishes, most nights we would end up sharing one single plate as we had dinner. Many people have been kind to me through their words but D heaped kindness on a plate that we shared together at a time where words no longer comforted me. His apartment kitchen was the birthplace of my meze table.

Since D loved to cook and feed his friends, some nights we would have friends over. We would all sit on the floor on a mat while sharing anecdotes and food. At some point, I seamlessly blended into the workforce of this kitchen that saw the creation of some of the most potent masalas as D researched the Hyderabadi biryani; other times as he experimented with homemade fruit ice creams, rasgullas and my favourite jalebis. If there is someone who invests in food as much as in friendship, it would be him. He welcomed me into his home and together we created this space where we invited many of our friends to share meals with us.

Our favourite friend was B. She had a sweet tooth that neither D nor I enjoyed. Her kind of sweet or her kind of alcohol was abhorrent to the both of us. So she decided it was a BYOB/S party. She brought her own stash of sickly-sweet chocolates and some fruity alcohol to stash in D's fridge. So every time she returned she didn't have to suffer through our non-sweet tooth lives. As the three of us cooked, we also spent hours working on our own writing or reading. I continued to speak in my broken Hindi-English, sometimes coupled with Tamil and French phrases. I even took naps between meals while D and B worked. D's food was laced with a special something that always had me asking for more or falling fast asleep.

It was on that floor that I built my meze table, with a little help from my friends. Here, we layered the chicken on top of a bed of rice (cooked 70 per cent only), coriander, mint, D's secret biryani masala, kewra water, ghee, saffron milk and fried onions. There is nothing more decadent than this biryani and nothing more fulfilling than sitting on the floor of his kitchen and layering the biryani together and sealing the vessel with dough so that the biryani cooks slowly in its own 'dum'. This tradition of marinating the meat the previous evening, frying the onions and layering the biryani together before enjoying it on our metaphoric meze table was a gift D gave to me when I needed it most.

This meze table didn't include platters of Mediterranean food, although we did have a raita to go with the biryani. This meze table slowly gave me back the gift of language. It allowed me to speak in English-Hindi-Tamil-French. This meze table set up on the floor of D's kitchen permitted me to forgive myself my linguistic sins and commit many a culinary sin. In the multilingual silence of this meze table, it finally dawned on me that the tongue is for more than just words; the tongue is for taste.

D's (NOT SO) SECRET HYDERABADI DUM BIRYANI RECIPE

Serves 4 to 6

Prepare the biryani masala one day in advance.

Biryani masala:

2 tbsp coriander seeds
2 tbsp black cumin
1 tbsp fennel seeds
1 tbsp stone flower
1 tbsp mace
3 star anise
3 kapok buds

2 bay leaves
2 cinnamon sticks
12 pods green cardamom
4 pods black cardamom
Half a nutmeg (save the other half to seep in the rice while cooking)

Recipe for biryani masala:

Dry roast all ingredients (in batches if need be). Do not burn them.
Once cool grind them to a powder and store in a cool dry container labelled D's secret biryani masala.

Marinade for ½ kg mutton:

(You can follow the same recipe with 800 gm of chicken minus the raw papaya paste)

1 tbsp ground raw papaya with skin
1 tbsp ginger-garlic paste
2 big onions ground into paste
5 green chillies
Handful of mint and coriander
350 ml yoghurt
Juice of two limes
1 tbsp of ghee
1 tsp of turmeric
Salt to taste
4 tbsp biryani masala

Recipe for marinade:

- Blend raw papaya, ginger-garlic paste, onions, chillies, mint and coriander into a fine paste. Don't smell it—it tickles the nose.

- Clean the meat thoroughly until the water runs clear.
- Add the blended mix to the meat along with curd, lime juice, ghee, turmeric, salt and biryani masala and incorporate well.
- Refrigerate overnight so the meat absorbs the spices.
- Next morning prep the following...

Ingredients for layering:

5 onions chopped lengthwise
Handful of mint leaves removed from stem
Handful of coriander leaves removed from stem
2½ cups of basmati rice
¼ glass warm milk, with a few threads of saffron mixed
    in for colour and flavour
1 tbsp biryani masala
4 tbsp ghee
2 tsp kewra water

Mutton and onion prep:

- Dump the mutton in a cooker and cook for four to six whistles with no added water based on the quality of the mutton.
- Slice the onions thin and long and shallow fry in three batches until they turn fully brown (don't forget to separate the onions into slivers).
- Remove onto a kitchen towel and allow it to crisp up.
- Once the steam releases from the cooker, check the consistency of the mutton gravy.
- If runny, heat again without the lid so the excess water evaporates.
- Meanwhile, begin to clean the rice and wash until water runs clear.

Spices to cook the rice:

2 green chillies
Half a nutmeg
5 cloves
1 cinnamon stick
2 mace
2 star anise
4 pods regular cardamom
2 pods black cardamom
½ tbsp stone flower

Recipe to cook the rice:

- Add the cleaned rice to a pot full of salted water along with the spices.
- Allow to cook 70 per cent (with a slight bite in the centre). Overcooking the rice at this stage will render the biryani mushy.
- Once the rice is cooked and the mutton gravy has reduced (reduce well, or the biryani will turn soggy) layering can begin.

Layering the biryani:

- Use a pot that is deep, thick and flat-bottomed so you can create many layers (at least three). Even a pressure cooker will do.
- For maximum satisfaction undertake layering of the biryani atop a mat on the floor of your kitchen with all the ingredients laid out with the help of friends or family (don't forget to bring your spoons before you sit down, you'll thank me for this detail later).
- Entrust each ingredient to one person. Involve all regardless of age or aesthetics in the process.

- Add 1 tsp ghee to the base of the pot you wish to cook the dum biryani in.
- Start by adding a small layer of rice followed by some biryani masala, a sprinkle of kewra water and saffron milk.
- Follow this with a layer of fried onion, coriander and mint.
- Atop this bed, lay your (not soggy) thick mutton gravy.
- Follow this with another layer of rice and repeat until the last layer which is only a layer of rice, onions, ghee, kewra water, saffron milk, coriander and mint without any meat.
- Shut the pot with a lid and seal the edges with wheat dough so that the steam does not escape from the pot. Use a stone mortar to weigh down the lid of the vessel along with the dough.
- You may also cook the biryani in a pressure cooker without using the whistle.
- Instead of the whistle use a small cap made of wheat dough to cover the whistle hole and cook for half an hour on low flame. Cooking on high flame will cause the lowest layer to burn and your makeshift dough whistle to burst.
- The biryani should be ready in 30 minutes.
- Serve with raita and enjoy at your meze table with loved ones. The effort is worth it.

Food is Life

Giles Duley

For fifteen years, I've been documenting conflicts. Photographing and listening to the stories of everyday people caught up in the brutal violence and madness that is war. Each one of those stories is like a scar on your memory, they never leave you. The child who lost his face when a mine exploded; the mother who watched her baby killed; the man who sits silent since the day his whole family was killed by a bomb that left no mark on him. And then one day the weight of those stories becomes so much you can't move, you become frozen.

That happened to me in early 2017, in Mosul, Iraq.

In October 2016 Iraqi and Kurdish forces, supported by US-led coalition airpower, had massed on the outskirts of the Mosul in preparation for an offensive to retake the city. Since June 2014 the city, Iraq's second biggest, had been under the violent rule of ISIS, the Islamic State of Iraq and Syria.

What followed was nine months of heavy street fighting. According to Lt. Gen. Stephen Townsend, the top coalition commander, it was the 'deadliest urban combat since World War II'. The US-led coalition, which included a dozen partner countries, carried out more than 1,250 air strikes on the city, hitting thousands of targets with over 29,000 munitions, according to official figures. ISIS themselves were sworn to fight to the death and planted thousands of Improvised Explosive Devices (IEDs) across the city. The civilian population found themselves trapped, unable to flee to safety.

The then US secretary of defence, James Mattis, described policy during the fight for Mosul as having 'shifted from attrition tactics, where we shove them from one position to another in Iraq and Syria, to annihilation tactics where we surround them…civilian casualties are a fact of life in this sort of situation.'

To this day nobody knows how many were killed in the fighting but thousands, tens of thousands, died. What is clear, when you speak to anybody who was in the city during the fighting, is that no family was untouched. As a resident said to me, 'There are over a million people living in Mosul, which means there are a million stories of loss. Nobody was spared.'

As the fighting reached a bloody climax in March 2017, I was based in a hospital run by the Italian NGO Emergency in Erbil, fifty miles from Mosul. Every day they received dozens of badly injured civilians from the fighting in the city. After over a decade of photographing the effects of conflict, the scenes I witnessed there were amongst the worst I'd seen. Babies with amputated limbs, whole families lost, a young child paralysed by a sniper's bullet. It was beyond words.

I believe photography comes with great responsibility, as soon as I lift my camera to record somebody's story; I have to ask myself 'why am I doing this?' Especially when that work is documenting another's suffering, nothing in photography goes more against human nature; the process of pointing your camera at somebody injured, afraid or in real peril. In the past I have referred to how I always try and find a positive in such situations, if possible a moment of humour, or to show the love between loved ones. But what I witnessed from Mosul left me beyond that; there are times you can find no such image.

I think of Firas. For four days I watched him silently as he sat by his son's bed. He nodded when I walked by, nothing more. Then one day he came over and grabbed my arm.

'It was not my fault,' he pleaded through dead eyes, a hollowed expression I have rarely seen, 'I did what I thought I was right.'

He then told me his story. How his family sheltered beneath a table in their home as bombs landed around them. The house opposite was hit, then the house next door. At that moment his nerve gave and he'd told his family they must run. As they left the front door, a third bomb smashed into them. Firas's wife, three daughters, two sons; all killed instantly. A son, Abdullah, left blind in one eye. Firas was untouched, not a scratch.

There is nothing one can say to such a story; you cannot say 'things will get better', for they never will. There is no hope or positive angle. This is the real face of war and its random, violent horror.

I photographed his son against a white wall, a patch still on his eye. Skin pitted by shrapnel, his expression as hollow as his father's.

I could only see the darkness and horror of what was happening. I was shooting angry, taking away my normal working practice of not showing the blood and gore. I wanted the world to see what was happening and to reel away as I had.

As the days passed, I knew this was wrong. It was not about me, it was about those I was photographing, and to do their stories justice, I had to work in a balanced way. I don't like the phrase to 'give people voice'; they have voices, my job is to make sure those voices are heard.

But still that question, why do it? What difference will a photograph make anyway? Only recently I'd heard my inspiration, the war photographer Don McCullin say there was no point in his years of work—because wars still go on. So if my photograph makes no difference, why point my camera at a child who's just been injured? It's an intrusive act and one that must have a purpose.

On the last day I was there, I sat with Dawood Salim, a 12-year-old boy who had lost both of his legs and most of his right hand. For the past week I'd been visiting him and his mother; he always smiled and joked. For the first time I felt ready to take his photograph.

I asked his mother, 'Do you mind if I photograph your son?'

She looked at me with a defiant yet resigned stare, 'When a child is injured like this, the whole world should see.'

Is that an answer to my doubts? Does that make it all okay? Of course not, but it reminds me of my simplest role, to act as witness, to tell their story. What Dawood's mother had said had not given me permission; it had challenged me to do what she had asked. There is no point in taking a photograph if I do not then do all I can to make sure the whole world sees it. That is where my duty lies.

I returned home broken: The culmination of stories, the

bleak reality of Mosul, the impotence of my camera to be able to stop the violence. I drew the curtains and drank to drown the noise of my own thoughts. It's normal for me to hit lows on returning from conflict areas, but this was deeper and darker than usual.

Having dealt with mental health issues my whole life, I knew where this course ran if I didn't fight it. I have learnt that I can never rid myself of that dark dog of depression, but over the years I've found ways to manage it, to tame it, to stop it from overwhelming me completely. This though was different, and I was struggling to open the curtains.

And then I started to cook.

I don't mean just prepare something to fill the void of hunger. No, I mean to make fresh pasta, to bake bread, start pickling, fermenting, all manner of long and complex recipes and techniques. I started to cook obsessively for hours at a time. Far more than I could consume. I left plates piled high outside my neighbours' flats.

When I was younger, I used to find my balance in running. Like everything I did, it was to an extreme. At one point I ran 150 miles across the Sahara to try and escape my own thoughts. But in 2011 an accident at work in Afghanistan had left me a triple amputee. Stepping on an IED whilst on foot patrol with the US 75th Cavalry Regiment, I lost both legs and an arm. I would never run again. It had left a void.

Reading a book or watching a film didn't help. My mind would still always race. Running had pushed me to my limits with its relentless rhythm, its focus on breathing, the exhaustion; all these things distracted me from my own thoughts.

Now I'd discovered cooking did the same and something

in my brain clicked when doing manual tasks such as kneading dough or shaping pasta. The concentration as I cooked a fillet of fish or presented a plate of food were moments when all I could think of was the moment itself—all other thoughts banished.

For a week I stayed at home, lost in my kitchen. Then slowly I started to re-engage with life. The scars healed. I wrote, edited my images from Mosul and prepared for my next trip. Somebody once asked the war photographer James Nachtwey how he could keep going back to war zones and their horrors. 'It's hard to witness these things, but once you have seen, it's even harder to turn your back.'

And that's the truth. I hate the things I photograph, but it's the only way I know how to speak out. To stop would be to fail those who have no choice, no opportunity to flee. Now though, when I return, I know to look for my peace in cooking.

In March 2018, a year after my previous visit, I returned to Mosul. The fight for the city was over; what was left was a wasteland. One day we drove through the shattered city to what once had been a thriving suburb of Mosul to visit Laila, an elderly woman who lived with her four grandchildren; Karim, Lama, Sari and Rami. In the neighbourhood there was hardly a building that wasn't damaged. The roads were cratered and filled with water from the smashed sewers and water pipes. Inside the house the walls were blackened; the acrid smell of smoke was still in the air, all possessions destroyed. The house looked like the set of some Hollywood war film.

When I arrived, Laila met me at the door. She was frantic, desperately trying to tell me her story. I couldn't even introduce myself. In her eyes I could see the grief, shock and trauma.

I pleaded for her to stop. 'Grandmother, you don't need to tell me your story, I have just come to visit.'

She continued, each word she spoke a memory of her pain.

'Please grandmother, listen to me for a moment, I would just like to cook with you.'

For a moment she stopped, confused as to why a one-armed man had travelled halfway around the world to a war zone just to cook with her!

'My grandmother was Italian,' I went on to explain, 'she taught me how to cook, but she is no longer with us, so I need a new grandmother to teach me. Can I come back tomorrow to visit? So we can cook together?'

For the first time she smiled, albeit puzzled, and nodded. I could return tomorrow.

Back in the car, the team told me the family's story. After years of oppressive, brutal ISIS control, the family waited for the liberation of their city. When the fight for the city began, they found themselves trapped on the frontlines as the fighting raged around them. The family sheltered in the basement. For four months they survived on potatoes and bulgur wheat. One day, the father went to the roof to collect water, as by now all utilities had ceased to work. As he collected water from the tank, he was killed by a missile strike.

Two days later, a mortar shell exploded in the garden killing the grandfather, Laila's husband. Karim, the eldest grandchild, was outside in the street. He ran back to the house to get help, and dragged his grandfather's body into the house. Inside he found shrapnel from the mortar shell had also hit his mother.

Under virtual siege by the fighting, they were unable to get help. Wounded in the stomach, Laila's daughter, the children's mother, died later that day. The blood stains were still visible on the kitchen floor.

A few days later a bomb hit the house next door, and the resulting fire spread. Soon their house was also ablaze, destroying the furniture and what possessions they had.

Now Karim must work as a porter to feed the family. His younger sister Lama stays home to cook and clean. They both accept their fate without complaint and will do whatever it takes to support what remains of their family and make sure their two younger siblings get an education. For them, like thousands of others in this city, their childhood is already over, cut short by war. For Laila, her health failing with age, she must now hold the family together.

The next day I returned with a frozen chicken and some rice, all I could find in the destroyed city. It turned out she was a terrible cook! We spent the next hour just trying to break up the chicken—in the end resorting to a hammer and chisel! But we laughed together, and for the rest of the day cooked and shared stories.

When it came time to eat, we sat together. Arabic food is all about sharing. Our hands were together in the rice and chicken. We sat silently, eating, smiling. All things considered, I'd have to say we did a pretty good job.

For me the difference between an acquaintance and a friend is the moment when we eat together. And as friendships were formed that day in the burnt-out room with its shattered windows, surrounded by ghosts, we all found our peace—for a moment.

And I was reminded that cooking and food is not just my therapy, it is also how I communicate and express my love. Food is life.

Recipe: Mujadara
(Lentils and Rice with Caramelised Onions)

Serves 5

Ingredients:

2½ cups green or brown lentils
1 cup rice
1 tsp salt
4 tbsp olive oil
6 onions—5 chopped, 1 sliced
1 tsp ground cumin
Black pepper
Parsley to serve

Method:

- Rinse lentils, strain and place in a large pot with 5 cups of water. Bring mixture to a boil, simmer and cook covered until the lentils are tender but not fully cooked, about 15 minutes. Most of the liquid should be absorbed.

- Rinse the rice, and then transfer to the pot of lentils and season with salt. Add 2 cups of water, bring to a boil, then reduce to a simmer and cook covered until the rice is tender, about 15 minutes. Remove the pot from the heat. Allow to rest for about 5 minutes, without opening the lid, to absorb all the liquid and steam.

- Meanwhile, warm two tablespoons of olive oil in a large skillet over medium-high heat and fry the chopped onions until golden brown, about 10 to15 minutes. Transfer on top of the lentils and rice mixture. Add cumin and pepper and mix gently with a fork.

- Add the rest of the olive oil to the same skillet over medium-high heat. Add the remaining (sliced) onions, stirring every couple of minutes to prevent burning. If the onions are browning before they have softened, dial down the heat to give them more time. Cook until the onions are caramelised and starting to crisp at the edges, about 20 to 30 minutes.
- Use a slotted spoon to transfer the onions to a plate lined with a paper towel and spread them evenly across. They'll crisp up as they cool.
- Put the caramelised onions on top of the mujadara. Garnish with chopped parsley and serve with sides of yoghurt and pickles.

Kadhi, Clutter and Grief

Shahana Raza

I've always had this deep compulsive need to control both my unruly curls and my unquiet mind till grief tipped the scales in its favour. Since then, I have searched for new methods to rebuild my emotional resilience—because the world with all its goodness has not been the same since 2003.

Clear the clutter, cook something.

It was not like the usual hospital gown. There was a slit, running all the way through the back which had to be closed with strings. I helped tie them in three places but could not find the pair for one errant string, curiously attached to a strange looking rectangular flap hanging midway down the back of the over-washed green gown.

'Mom, maybe this gets wrapped around you,' I said, placing the flap and lone string impatiently in her hand before walking off towards the bed.

Amma stood in the middle of the hospital room looking baffled. 'No, no, we've done something wrong...let's do it again slowly...Achcha look...'

I turned back and saw my mother holding the solitary string attached to that bizarre piece of cloth delicately between her index finger and thumb, as if it were the tail of a gorgeous long ballroom gown.

We both laughed.

Amma cleared her throat dramatically and started humming a happy sort of tune. Then sucking her cheeks in like a model she began strutting up and down the room. She cat-walked the length of the room, threw her head back for effect, paused, posed, turned around, then walked all the way back. All this in her knee-length surgery gown, barefoot, with a medical cannula inserted in her forearm. I laughed so loud the nurse had to rush in to ask me to stop disturbing the other patients.

It was five o'clock in the morning.

Stifling her giggles, Amma asked the nurse, 'Sister, is there something wrong with this gown? See this piece of cloth? We don't know where it goes.'

Sister, who had absolutely no sense of humour, reprimanded her for prancing around the room. 'Please go lie down. I will get another gown,' she said in her thick colloquial accent.

Amma and I doubled with laughter at her reaction and tried to suppress our noisy cackles as tears rolled down our faces. As soon as the nurse left, Amma cheekily did one more ramp walk for me, then went and lay down. That was so like my mother. She could find humour in any situation.

Later that morning, the doctor came on his rounds and said they could not do the scheduled kidney stone operation. Amma was delighted.

'So, I'm okay now, Doctor sahab? Did the stones come out?'

He smiled. 'We hope they do. We have to postpone the surgery today as your blood platelet count is very low.'

She didn't get it. Medically Amma was a toothless baby. I was beginning to frown.

He went on, 'We will have to run some blood tests, see why this is happening and then proceed.'

'Do I have to stay in hospital till then?' Amma asked.

'No, you can go home for now.'

'Oh, thank you Doctor!' she exclaimed. 'Uff, I can't wait to get out of here. Your dietician gives such bad food. I would like to meet her and give her a few tips on making food tastier for sugar patients. I mean Doctor sahab, just because we have diabetes, does not mean we have to be given badmaza khana, such insipid tasteless food. She can lightly sauté lauki sabzi with garlic and ajwain (carom seeds) in just a teaspoon of oil to add flavour to the bottle gourd...'

She would have carried on and on about food and recipes, but the doctor told her politely he had to see other patients. I followed him down the corridor to ask the important question.

'What is wrong with my mother's blood picture, Doctor?'

This was 7 October 2003.

By 23 October, Amma left for the US to get treated for ALL: Acute Lymphoblastic Leukaemia, a rare galloping cancer which claimed my mother, Naushaba's life, within two swift weeks of detection. She was only fifty-seven years old and not prepared to go. Not to God or even to the United States. The only place she really wanted to be, was back home in Lucknow.

'Sherry, send me for one day, beta.'

I refused. 'Mom you know you cannot. You have to be kept away from crowds. Airport lounges are filled with sneezing-wheezing passengers. Not to mention all those dogs and cats you have in the house. We cannot have you contracting any sort of infection before chemotherapy. As it is, your diabetes is not under control...'

'Even God gives a day, Sherro,' she retorted disappointedly, as she filed her nails for the nth time.

But I am not sure that's true. Amma never came home.

Amma passed away due to pulmonary oedema after just two sessions of chemo. While her blood cells kept multiplying healthily, the capillaries in her lungs were bursting, filling rapidly with blood. The machines she was hooked up on whirred loudly as the damn respirator made futile attempts to pump air into her lungs. But the volume of fluid in her lungs would not let her breathe.

It just seemed like Amma's time was up. She had to go. And she did. Without making any sad defeatist dialogues and without hiding her compulsive desire to live.

Her death brought an end to thirty-three years of my life.

There are days I wake up and find myself back in that hospital room. By evening, I am praying to God to forgive me and help me walk out. There is a world waiting outside which I am learning to embrace and come to terms with. A world without her, a world with less acceptance. A world I must learn to tackle daily. I pray for emotional release.

Clear the clutter, cook something.

In the initial days after Amma, there was despair and a dense choking feeling, as though nothing would ever be right. My firstborn child was only eleven months old. Her presence would draw me back to reality. In those early days of grief, I remember trying to cook various sophisticated dishes I would not have thought of attempting earlier. I tried my hand at Amma's delicious kofta. Soft and crumbly, the meatballs went to pieces the minute I placed them in the thick aromatic gravy. The kofta looked like mush.

Amma was a fabulous cook. We used to call her 'Leftover Queen'. She could skilfully transform the previous day's leftovers—veggies or meat—into a tasty new dish completely unlike the original!

The first recipe I feel I so-called 'mastered' after she passed away was kingfish, coated in a thick besan (gram flour) batter, deep-fried in piping hot mustard oil. It had to be marinated the night before in some masalas which I can't remember now.

I have, since, lost that recipe.

Any dish made with besan is soul food for me. In fact, Amma innovatively fused together two versions of kadhi before she arrived at the kind I relish most today—a unique blend of the simple Punjabi besan ki kadhi found in any dhaba across Delhi and the kind cooked and enjoyed in homes throughout North India.

Besan, also referred to as chane ka atta, is an extremely versatile legume. There is a delightful historical anecdote about it that dates back to 1659. When Emperor Aurangzeb imprisoned his own father, Shah Jahan, who had the Taj Mahal built, in Agra Fort, he asked the former king to choose one food grain for himself as he would have to eat only that for the rest of his life. The foresighted Shah Jahan wisely chose chana.

Chana or chickpea can be prepared as daal or chole. Add this daal to meat or nutri-nuggets and you can dish up various appetising items including vegan and non-veg kababs. Pound it fine into powder and use this besan to make a delicious savoury pancake called cheela or deep-fried fritters, popularly known as pakoras. Heat chana with ghee, add oodles of sugar, cook over a slow fire and you get a delectable sweet dish called chane ka halwa. Even the leaves of the chana plant can be sautéed with chopped garlic and eaten as a stand-alone vegetable dish.

As years have passed, writing, clearing clutter and cooking have proved extremely cathartic in helping me deal with my inconsistent anxiety and unrelenting grief. I have come to understand that rage is another avatar of grief which I have consciously, and at times unsuccessfully, battled almost every day of my life, flaring up if I find shoes flung around the house, books tossed on wet counters or noisy, irritating toys squealing loudly under my feet.

I wrote my mother letters and poems and posted them to myself. 'Remember the ring we bought together in Sunder Nagar. Which you loved and didn't want to get but I convinced you to? It makes me sad as it was for you, it was yours, you should be wearing it. But along with so many of your other rings and earrings, bits and bobs, it is now sadly mine.'

> In the letter I write to you
> I say I am better now. Much better.
> They are the wrong words.
> Lilac is the love I feel.
> Red is the pain.
> I paint memories of you
> in multiple shades of both.
> The picture is a mess
> much like my mind.
> Silent lines tangled,
> blind strokes moving
> in any which direction.
> From a distance,
> the complete picture looks peaceful.
> Don't get too close.

Cooking has worked like balm. Even though I am impatient by nature and cannot, c-a-n-n-o-t wait for the oil to be hot enough before I toss in the rai (mustard) or zeera (cumin) seeds. I have devised coping mechanisms to help deal with this aspect of my inherent nature.

Put oil in the pan, throw in the rai (or zeera). Start washing and chopping the other food items such as onions, tomatoes or ginger-garlic. Buy time till the oil heats up. This works! It checks the urge to add ingredients to lukewarm oil. I've also learnt to use lids; they expedite the heating process. What also helps is choosing no-fuss recipes. I gravitate towards dishes that can be prepared in record time. Multiple steps in detailed methods of cooking are too overwhelming, even if the end result is a mouth-watering biryani or a delicious qorma.

One needs to save energy to clean up. Whether it is the countertop, the chopping board or the stove, for me, clearing up must go hand in hand with cooking. It is absolutely sacrosanct.

Does this make me (borderline) OCD?

When I was working and living by myself in New Delhi, the popular American sitcom *Friends* was all the rage. I was often referred to as Monica Geller—the friend best known for her fastidious obsessive-compulsive nature. In my teens, I would sort out my friends' messy cupboards. At that age, we shared outfits and if I could sort and fold their clothes during our enjoyable day-spends together, why not?

As a child, I battled to tame my curls. Kinky hair looks amazing once combed and set. But curls don't know how to cooperate. They have to be coaxed down with potent serums, leave-in conditioners, frizz-ease creams, lock-down gels—a whole battalion of products before victory can be yours.

At eight I went to boarding school. Before joining, I had two tight plaits which hung neatly below my shoulders. Back home, the maids would often complain while combing my hair, but it was the incessant grumbling from the matrons— 'Oh Mrs Raza, it takes us twice the time to brush Shahana's hair, the other children keep waiting their turn and get late for breakfast'—that convinced my mother to cut my hair short. Real short.

I'm sure I cried. It's a memory I have deliberately erased. What I do remember is walking into the hostel and being called 'white golliwog'. I had an Afro cut much like Michael Jackson's in *Off the Wall.*

As my hair grew back, I knew it was time to take charge and learn once and for all how to take care of my own curls. No ayahs. No matrons. Slowly and painfully I brushed my tangled hair, created a parting of sorts, held my frizzy curls in place with several bobby pins as I bunched one side of my hair carefully into a small ponytail and quickly twirled a rubber band on it. At times the flimsy rubber bands would snap and sting my hands, but I was determined. Little did I know that as my ponytails grew, they would defy gravity. The next moniker I had the pleasure of enduring was 'junior school poodle'. Getting a job meant freedom from rubber bands and clips. One could pay and get those curls straightened, despite the long-term damage it did to my pocket and my hair.

After coming back from boarding school, I started baking cakes. Most were pretty decent though once I turned a lemon sponge cake into a weird bile-green colour. God alone knows how!

Whenever life gets a bit overwhelming I move into the kitchen. I have gone to my friends' homes and cooked for them.

 Shahana Raza

Clear the clutter, cook something.

Reprogramming what I call my borderline Obsessive Compulsive Disorder has been somewhat of an ongoing uphill task. Uphill mainly because I can see the traits that could tip me over, and keep realigning the balance. Dust and dirt does not bother me as much as having things strewn around the house does. Scissors, knives, packets, paper, tissue, cordless phones…pencils…the urge to put things back where they belong, is overpowering, especially since I had my two children. I know many homemakers who are also sticklers for 'put it back where you got it from', hence the use of the word 'borderline'. And also because none of these emotional battles raging within have stopped me from achieving any of my goals—personal, professional or daily.

My OCD symptoms settle in somewhere near repeatedly checking to see if my children are safe (over the years I've devised methods of tackling this), having compelling thoughts of doom and death at the slightest sneeze, and the absolute inability to endure clutter. When the compulsion to call the children again and again repeats itself, I distract myself with long walks, phone calls to good friends and brewing a strong cup of gud-chai—black tea with jaggery, the exact shade of caramelised brown-black that is visually appealing and which satiates my caffeine craving.

Unashamedly undiagnosed and happy to plod on with whatever syndrome is now moving along with me over the fifty-year threshold, I have made peace with grief (it's here to stay) and I am calmed by the thought that every house comes equipped with a kitchen.

Recipe: Besan ki Kadhi

Kadhi is a North Indian dish, best enjoyed with plain white rice.

Serves 4 to 5

Ingredients:

Mustard oil
Fenugreek (methi) seeds
Onion—chopped
Ginger-garlic paste
Tomato—chopped
Dry spices—turmeric (haldi), red chilli and coriander
Yoghurt
Besan (gram flour or chickpea flour) powder
For the tempering:
Ghee
Mustard seeds (rai)
Whole red chilli
Curry leaves (kadi patta)
Asafoetida powder (hing)
Red chilli powder
For the pakoras (fritters):
Onions, tomatoes coriander leaves and green chillies
or
Potato and cauliflower

Method:

- Mix together two tablespoons of besan flour with one and half cups of yoghurt and half cup of water. Whip thoroughly. Keep aside.

- Pour mustard oil into a deep saucepan or wok.
- Smoke the oil with a sliver of onion to temper its bitterness.

Add

- 5-6 fenugreek seeds (methi dana) and let them brown slightly.
- Add half of the onion—finely chopped, sauté till it turns pink.
- Add 1 tablespoon ginger-garlic paste.
- Along with half teaspoonful each of the dry powders—turmeric, chilli and coriander (reduce chilli powder if you don't like it very spicy).
- Keep stirring and cooking masala with little bit of water till it starts to leave oil.
- Add half a tomato—finely chopped or grated (skinless is better).
- Cook these together till all the oil starts coming to the surface in small pools.
- Sprinkle water if the mixture starts sticking to the bottom of the pot.
- Add the besan and yoghurt mixture to the oil, stir and let it cook till it boils.
- Then lower flame, add salt, cook on medium heat till a thin film of oil appears on top.

For the tempering or tadka:

- Put half teaspoon rai (mustard seeds) in hot ghee.
- After they splutter, break and add one whole dry red chilli.
- Add washed kadi patta (curry leaves) along with a pinch of hing (asafoetida) powder.
- When everything has crackled and sizzled, add a quarter

teaspoon of red chilli powder and immediately remove the tadka from heat.
- Pour slowly over cooked kadhi.

Prepare a variety of fritters:
- Mix half a teaspoon of baking soda to a cup of besan powder.
- Add in quarter teaspoons of turmeric powder, chilli powder (optional) and salt.
- Add water to this mixture till it thickens to a consistency like pancake batter.
- Chop up onions, tomatoes, green chillies (optional) fresh coriander and mix into batter.
- Heat mustard oil and fry the fritters till golden brown.
OR
- Make simple vegetable pakoras by cutting potatoes into thin round slices or cauliflower into bite-size florets, dip them in besan batter and fry till golden brown.
- You can add these delicious fried pakoras to the kadhi or serve them on the side.

Becoming Kintsugi through Reclaiming My Broken Selves

Tikuli

When I look back to all the years I have felt isolated, hurt, depressed or abused in some way, I realise that my time in the kitchen has healed and grounded me in ways that can't be quantified. Food wasn't the only thing that helped me battle positively with my circumstances and struggles. I wasn't being medically treated for anything but coping with my mental and emotional demons felt harder every time I thought of conquering them. So I befriended most of them. They were there, as real as I was and perhaps played the role of friends and foes as I let them.

Cooking wasn't the main focus in my earlier years. I found comfort in eating, but it wasn't binge eating. I had very specific dishes for specific ways I was feeling. They weren't planned; I just knew what I was craving. If it was love and warmth then the go-to dish would be a simple 'mumum', a toasted, buttered bread pudding made on a gas stove, an apple stew if it was winter, or a bowl of khichdi topped with ghee, to name a few. When I was hurt or angered, I would steal the raw tamarind or anything else that was prohibited for me as it was being kept for my elder brother.

My growing-up years were full of mental-emotional trauma I did not understand beyond the shame, hurt and loneliness they caused. With no one to turn to, I would fill myself with the cold or warmth of food that I could curl up and eat, in the solitude of my room or in the emptiness of a house which never felt like home. Even the pleasant memories of reading to my mother, or playing antakshari (the game of singing with the ending letter) while she cooked were seared with images I wanted to forget. In such times I craved meat dishes I could debone while eating. However, we were a vegetarian household and seldom got food from outside so it filled me with a rage that resulted in a backlash or tears until I could get hold of a knife to chop vegetables, fruits or go out to eat some non-vegetarian dish (which was rare). I think it saved me from self-harm though it didn't sustain me. I learned to cook and actually relish non-vegetarian dishes much later.

On most occasions, our kitchen wasn't the sanctuary I wanted to escape to, food was. On the other hand, I loved spending hours in other kitchens including community kitchens like gurudwaras, or in those of my friends' homes. There was something very comforting in watching food being prepared from scratch: The raw ingredients, the aromatic steam rising from curries and lentils, the rhythmic sound and movement of grinding stone, the chopping of seasonal produce, the sizzle of spices in hot pans. Everything seemed more relaxing to watch than the actual eating. I longed for that comfort for many years. When I tried to bring it to our kitchen I failed, or so I thought. I cooked to rebel. It was something I wanted control over, perhaps as a reaction to being controlled all my life. I rejoiced in the fact that there was something that I had gained control over and succeeded. It was later that I realised it was a passion more than anything else, a passion for bringing back my dignity, self-esteem, self-belief, and self-love.

Things changed in my early twenties when I got married. Even though I wasn't 'allowed' in the kitchen most of the time, I knew I had found my linchpin. I watched my mother-in-law cook day in and day out, lamenting over her misfortune of having me as a daughter-in-law. In that process, I learned the secrets of a cuisine different to ours. Here, in this kitchen, I found how much I wanted to cook for others more than just myself. I began relishing the scrumptious, rustic, Punjabi meals and found opportunities to include our side of recipes too. In those many years, I believe one of the things that kept my broken pieces and spirit together was cooking. It helped me cope with all that was wrong. Not that it cured anything but it certainly helped alleviate depression and social anxiety. It was personally rewarding and gave me a sense of the accomplishment and joy that I yearned for. It gave me a sense of well-being too because I wasn't cooking what's termed as 'unhealthy'. I also gradually began to distinguish craving from need. Sometimes a craving would hit me hard and I would recognise it as a reaction to something nasty happening to me that day or maybe to a memory of an equally disturbing event from the past, throwing me into a whirlwind. At times like these, I would cook a laborious dish, giving it all of my energy and love, and feed my children, friends, and whoever I thought would appreciate and encircle me with those invisible arms of affection. It helped me reclaim myself.

I never saw or used cooking as 'therapy' as I never liked boxing things under labels but it certainly boosted my skills and confidence. Fortunately, my boys loved the entire process from kitchen to table and enjoyed the different meals I served. This became one of the foundations of our bonding and our love. To a large extent, it healed my childhood trauma. I guess I lived my girlhood again with my children in a more fulfilling way.

It is important to mention something here; I wasn't raised like most Indian girls. Cooking wasn't a compulsion or an 'every girl must learn and excel to please the husband and in-laws' for me as it is for millions of Indian girls. It was a choice I made. One of the many I was determined not to give up. Cooking wasn't just about creating or feeding, it was about 'choices', about asserting myself, about finding my voice. It was a lifesaver, and still is.

I still find focus for writing and the other things I do by churning up something in the kitchen. Whether it is instant or elaborate depends on my level of anxiety or stress. Physically, mentally and emotionally involving myself in making something becomes more therapeutic than the meal itself. Even in a dense brain fog, I'm able to cook without getting stressed. Perhaps my hands have a memory of their own so the mental fog doesn't affect them. They have a way of guiding the mind into pure focus.

Self-healing is messy—it has its setbacks, pain, failures, and it certainly takes longer—but it is very rewarding. I have come a long way from being a hungry observer to sharing recipes and my experiences with others through my blog and social channels. It fills me with immense joy and satisfaction when someone else finds his/her linchpin through me. I have come to understand how cooking for others has been a defining moment in my struggle to recover and reclaim myself. In the last many years, a dish gone wrong has only motivated me to work harder rather than leaving me feeling helpless and inadequate. At the same time, each perfect creation becomes an extension of who I am.

There are times when I am physically incapable of cooking what I would want but even then I step into the kitchen, reaffirming my resolve not to let my mind control me. It is a difficult task but not unachievable, unlike other times when I am totally at the mercy of my mind playing tyrant. In fact, I find that shifting the focus from my physical or mental ailment, getting physically involved in making something from scratch, allows me breathing space, a way to think and to collect my thoughts. It helps me revive my spirits and helps me to move, one step at a time. It provides me with a sense of identity however transient. For that time I am in control. It helps me find who I am.

The different food I prepare has a different effect on me. Now I know eating specific foods will help me in specific situations. I'm more aware of eating mindfully too. For example, fermented food including home-cultured yoghurt, homemade pickles, kimchi, even idlis, help calm my anxiety. Whenever I am a bundle of nerves, which is often these days due to hormonal upheaval, I eat one of my fermented dishes. It helps soothe my parasympathetic nervous system or simply my gut. And the feeling of discomfort passes.

I have experienced it also works like a charm when I am going through social anxiety. One of the reasons I love dahi poha, or for that matter, curd rice immensely, is because it is nourishing and full of prebiotics and probiotics. It has gotten me out of stressful days like magic. I eat yoghurt if I am anxious before heading out for something important or have a long day ahead. I include my instant water-based seasonal pickles or mustard fermented instant pickles in daily meals to get more raw, seasonal produce on my plate. Pickling is a comforting art that I especially enjoy because they are healthier than those off the shelf, and more delicious too.

I also read a lot about healing through food and cook accordingly most of the time. That doesn't mean I don't indulge but I don't call it cheat eating. One of the things I have learned is to cook and eat with acceptance and gratitude. Cooking helped me to be present, grateful and loving to myself and thus maybe to others. Perhaps this was one of the reasons the older generations recited mantras or prayers before and while cooking, blessing the food and being thankful for receiving and giving. Somewhere I feel, the energy we put into what we cook and eat heals us and makes us who we are. There is a saying in Hindi, 'jaisa tann waisa mann' (like body, like mind). One could say it works both ways.

Now, in my mid-fifties, I crave things associated with those very few happy times spent at my maternal grandmother's or friends' homes while I was growing up or when my boys were growing up. I cook to keep that fragile link to my culinary past alive. Bringing traditional recipes to the public, preparing them for family and friends and of course for myself, trying to find a quicker yet equally tastier version for those who love to eat something nourishing or traditional but can't cook due to lack of knowledge or time, finding purpose in it all. In my daily struggle to live with as much contentment as possible, I still find time to paint, write, wander off to places I want to visit, all the time keeping all the broken pieces of myself joined beautifully together like kintsugi, which is the Japanese art of repairing broken pottery with lacquer mixed with gold or silver.

RECIPE: INSTANT RED CARROT PICKLE

This instant pickle can be eaten within a day of making it. One can add a few slit fresh green chilies to it if desired. It will give the pickle a beautiful red and green colour.

Usually this pickle can stay up to a week in the fridge. I make a small quantity of fresh pickle as carrots are inexpensive and easily available all through the winter months.

Ingredients:

½ kg medium size carrots
1½ tsp salt (to taste)
2 tsp full coarsely ground mustard seeds
1 tsp red chilli powder
½ tsp turmeric powder
A good pinch or ⅛ tsp asafoetida
2 tbsp lemon juice
2 tbsp mustard oil

Method:

- Wash and peel the carrots under fresh running water. Pat them dry and cut into 2- inch long thin juliennes. Place a kitchen napkin or kitchen towel on a tray and arrange the julienned carrots on it to dry. Make sure that no water remains or the pickle will become rancid. Sometimes I pat them with a damp cloth to clean instead of washing.
- You can leave it overnight or for instant pickle just keep in the sun for two hours or so. Cover it with thin muslin cloth to prevent any dust particles settling on the carrots.

- Once the carrots are absolutely dry, put them in a glass bowl. Add all the ingredients one by one except the oil. Squeeze the juice of half a lemon and mix well.
- Mix properly. (At each stage make sure your hands and the utensils you use are clean and dry.)
- Heat mustard oil in a heavy bottom pan till it begins to smoke. Turn off the flame and let it come to a warm temperature. (If you are using olive oil then there is no need to heat it. Just add it along with other ingredients in the bowl and mix well).
- Add all the ingredients to it and stir well.
- Let the pickle cool properly.
- Take a glass or stone jar. Wipe it clean and spoon the pickle in it.
- Keep the pickle in the sun for a day and it is ready to eat.
- This mustard-spiked carrot pickle goes well with anything from curd rice to parathas and even sandwiches. You can make it fresh and toss it in a salad too but in that case, use olive oil in it.
- Preserve the colours of winter in the jar and open the lid to brighten up a dull morning.

Balancing Life's Flavours

Kriti Dheer

Whenever I think back to my childhood, I don't see much of a carefree self, just laughing away, enjoying the moment. Although, on a harder second glance, there were some enjoyable times—running around the house playing with my younger siblings, fun birthday parties, sleepovers with friends, weekend family picnics, watching *Tom & Jerry* with my nani while eating the cheese toast, cakes, caramel pudding she so fondly made, eating some of my other favourites made by Ma, outings with my maasi and some other bits. So, no, it wasn't all bad! But there are specific vivid memories which do come rushing back—me crying at a new nursery school being consoled by my class teacher on multiple occasions, me crying because my best friend stopped coming to school for a bit or having a falling out with friends, my inability to cope at the age of twelve with not having my mother around as she went back to her professional life or being paralysed by fear, unable to focus at all, in the wake of approaching tests and exams; my experience or rather experiences of learning how to swim were also painted with the exact same emotions and reactions (I never did learn). But it wasn't as simple as feeling better after a good cry. These reactions were physiological. Any unnerving event would also lead me to having a complete loss of appetite and constant bouts of throwing up. And it would take me a long time and a lot of effort to wind back down to the state of being functional. These 'episodes' were pretty frequent till I completed my master's degree.

What was this feeling that took over me so vehemently? As a child, I was scared and confused. I didn't understand what was going on; neither did my parents or teachers. Over a period of time, my family and I came to accept these 'reactions' as something that were an inherent part of my life, my nature. I would get triggered, struggle, get through it somehow and move on. It was exhausting to say the least. Later in life, one of my therapists rightly pointed out that my symptoms/ reactions/ emotions were always only managed, never dealt with. Since then it's been an ongoing process.

Eventually this 'feeling' was diagnosed as anxiety. I can never forget one such episode which took a huge toll on me but also really shook my parents. I was triggered by a weekly physics test (I hadn't prepared in advance and the test was in two days) which cascaded into a major nervous breakdown. Feelings of panic, breathlessness, constant queasiness and throwing up on repeat led to my becoming incredibly weak. I was not eating, I refused to go to school and constantly cried. I was fourteen years old! I had, in fact, experienced all of this before but never with such virulence. My mental and emotional condition further worsened, and I felt useless, devoid of confidence, hopeless and scared. That incident was a blaring loudspeaker, screaming for help towards my mental wellbeing. Medical tests indicated nothing was wrong with me physically. It was then that my parents were told to take me to a psychiatrist. Well, surprise, surprise—the anxiety was accompanied with a generous dose of depression. For the first time, I and more so my parents, became aware of the fact that there was a problem, a problem concerning my mental health. Although I'm not sure what they felt about it at the time and definitely lacked guidance on this 'vague' subject, they did the best they could under the circumstances. I finished school, my Bachelor's and my Master's, all the while managing my anxious and depressive episodes as they occurred (I was taking some homeopathy medication too).

Living with anxiety and depression hasn't allowed me to learn many skills that I would have wanted to at various stages of my life; it hasn't allowed me to think logically and clearly on various occasions, or to make well-informed decisions (even the most trivial ones like shopping for clothes). I have stopped myself from living many experiences for the fear that something might go wrong or simply because I don't believe I can handle those wonderful, challenging experiences, despite knowing in my heart how much I needed them or would have enjoyed them. It has hampered my ability to trust in myself. It has pervaded and limited my daily life for years. But the most glaring impact that has been created in my life as a result is not having a 'career path'. Having completed my Master's in 2010, I got a job, where I stuck it out for a year and a half. All this time, I was going through a major depressive episode. When I quit, to move on to a new job, I was caught off guard. My mind was suddenly plagued with questions, starting with why did I not feel passionate enough about my job like others around me, had I made a mistake choosing my profession? How could I rectify that? Despite evidence to the contrary, I had convinced myself that I just wasn't capable enough to handle challenges at the workplace. And so I never went into my new place of work—what I thought would be a small break from work lasted five years!

All of this led to a breakdown and an existential crisis—what was the purpose of my life? Why was it that suddenly I had no clue about what I wanted to do with my life, something people around me seemed to be doing seamlessly? What was I so afraid of? I felt trapped in a maze, wandering aimlessly, constantly running into dead ends. For some reason (not known to me even now) my anxiety had gotten specifically attached to my professional life, and my depression was being fuelled more by me not having a career and measuring myself against societal standards. During this time, I got married and moved into my partner's home—living with his parents, abiding by new house rules, surrounded by a different, more formal set of relationships—and I am grateful to my partner for making this life-altering transition easy for me.

During the course of those five years, I did apply for jobs. At times I got rejected. The jobs that I did get, I quit within the very first week owing to low self-confidence, anxiety regarding managing work and home and just a plain lack of belief in my abilities. This led to me feeling unprofessional (when I am actually the complete opposite) and guilty for not being 'productive' and contributing financially towards the life that I wanted to build with my partner, putting all that pressure on him. I was clouded by a sense of disappointment in myself because I felt like I was letting my family and friends down. My batchmates/ friends had moved towards greener pastures, earning significant salaries, travelling, starting families—living their lives to the fullest. Here I was, stuck in the silent trap of comparing my life with others, mastering the recipe of self-loathing. I was stuck in a loop because everywhere I went, the first questions thrown at me were: Where are you working? Or, what do you do? Is your husband doing well enough, can you afford to not be working? Followed by advice on what might 'help'. I was also labelled as being lazy and complacent.

Like an unwanted relative who visits more often than you'd like, my anxiety and depression continued to loom over my head, making their presence known with all the noise they created in my head.

Being the eldest of three siblings and a child of working parents, I had learnt how to make basic things like chai, rice, khichdi, raita, eggs and of course Maggi! There were those once-in-a-blue-moon exercises of pulling out a recipe from one of my mum's cookbooks and giving it a go, but mostly for fun. At some point during my anxiety-induced sabbatical from work (after my very first job), I discovered that 'joy of cooking' and my surprisingly good culinary skills. My first major attempt was a peanut butter chocolate cake I had made for my partner's birthday. It looked average because I had never iced a cake before but it tasted delicious. I gradually started taking recipes from my mother, aunt, nani, mother-in- law (all of them exceptional cooks, by the way), and began to cook. I realised it gave me a sense of achievement, albeit minor, and the validation made me feel good.

What started out as a need for approval and an activity to occupy my mind, developed into a journey of introspection and discovery. I find joy in cooking not because I can master a recipe (although the satisfaction that brings is hard to ignore) but because of the person I become whilst completely immersed in the process. I am calm, confident and in control—I know exactly what to do, how to do it and that the outcome will be good (at least 95 per cent of the time!).

One struggle of living with anxiety and depression, and one I think many people with the same condition would relate to, is that of swinging between living in the past (regretting/ blaming), and being scared of the uncertainty of the future. I realised I was rarely 'present'. At most times this makes it challenging for me to focus on and give complete attention to the task at hand because I am drawing the worst conclusions about the outcome based on my perception of my abilities or how things have turned out in the past. I am easily distracted by my circumstances, and a constant critical inner dialogue, which more often than not is counterproductive. I have, however, with the help of certain practices and changes in my life, learnt to circumvent this obstacle over the years.

But when I started to cook I discovered, surprisingly so, that my mind for that duration was quiet and engrossed. There was a clarity that I wasn't quite used to, with my eyes set on a goal of preparing a delicious meal. My mind was focused, and it wouldn't waver, even in the wake of the occasional burnt dish or finger cut or the shortage of an ingredient. I was able to take these setbacks in my stride and improvise. Although this ease took some time to develop, it just took a rather natural, seamless course. Cooking also gave me the opportunity to be creative and challenge myself in ways that I enjoyed. Knowing that I was good at it, of course gave me that ego boost. I had uncovered a new skill and finally, a passion.

Cut to me in my kitchen, with music playing in the background (mostly). My prep begins. From the moment I collect my ingredients, wash the vegetables, and choose my cooking utensils, my process of engagement starts, even with these seemingly mundane tasks. The entire atmosphere of my kitchen slowly turns into a sensory experience—the smell of fresh ginger-garlic paste, chillies and cumin being tempered in ghee or a freshly baked cake wafting through the kitchen, hearing the whistle of the cooker or the sizzle of dropping something in hot oil, kneading the dough with my hands or chopping vegetables with precision or even burning my hand (a friend and I jokingly call kitchen mishaps 'injuries' or 'scars of battle') and watching the entire process tended to with love, amalgamating into a creation that is beautiful and nourishing. And of course, the part of the process most looked forward to is when I sit with my family, friends and occasionally even alone to savour that plate full of goodness.

Cooking has become an anchor for my senses, allowing me to channel my energies without distractions. It is a time when my body and mind both are at ease, working together rhythmically, restoring balance to what at times feels like living in a lopsided reality. While cooking, I become a person who is happy, passionate, confident and hopeful— what I constantly long to feel. Cooking has also made me more mindful about food—I am grateful for and respect the produce I consume (and cook with), along with being a wonderful opportunity for me to look more closely at my own physical well-being.

Additionally, cooking for me is about making people smile. I love hosting parties, feeding my family and friends till they are stuffed, which gives me the ultimate high. And now as a mama, I am exploring food in a completely new way with my little boy. It is definitely a way for me to give the people in my life that little extra dose of TLC. Oh, talking about loving food and cooking, I have to mention my love for the series, *Master Chef Australia*! On a side note though, I have also discovered that doing freelance film projects, for now, are a much better fit for me.

Coping with anxiety and depression is a journey—there are both good and bad days, wins and losses. According to me, it is best explained as a conscientious effort towards unlearning, discovering and finding ways to alchemize with various forces in your daily life. However, mental health challenges aside, practicing healthy habits towards self-care is a necessary investment for everyone's mental well-being. Cooking is an act of self-care for me. Added to that, the love and support of my family and friends, therapy, spending time with my cat babies, being outdoors in nature, yoga and meditation are equally important ingredients of a near perfect blend, I use, every day, to do my best.

RECIPE: BURMESE KHOW-SUEY

Note: I decided to share this recipe because it is the first thing that I made successfully when I started to cook. It's certainly a crowd-pleaser, much loved by my friends and family. A wholesome meal, it can easily be made for an intimate dinner/ lunch setting for up to eight people. This is not an original recipe, but a combination/ derivative of several recipes of the dish that I have come across. It's a bit labour-intensive, but easy to make. The entire process amalgamates into a meal which is healthy, comforting and a celebration of flavours on your palette.

Serves 2-3

Ingredients:

For the curry:

2 whole dried red chillies
1 large sprig curry leaves
600 ml coconut milk
1 tsp cumin powder
1 tsp coriander powder
½ tsp turmeric powder
Salt to taste
250 gm spaghetti/ egg noodles/ Hakka noodles

For the condiments:

1 large onion / 1 cup sliced onions
10 garlic cloves, sliced
½ cup unsalted peanuts (without skin)
5 to 6 green chillies
2 eggs
2 lemons
200 gm mushrooms
1 medium-sized broccoli
1 small zucchini
¼ cup vegetable oil

Method:

1. **Preparing the condiments:**

- Eggs—hard-boiled, cut into 4 quarters (if pure vegetarian, you can leave the eggs out),
- Green chillies—finely sliced.
- Lemon—cut into 4 wedges each.

- Peanuts—lightly roasted and crushed roughly.
- Vegetables—Chop mushrooms into fours, zucchini into cubes, separate broccoli florets and cut them into medium-sized pieces. To cook, separately sauté each vegetable in minimal oil till cooked, keep aside.
- (You can use any other vegetables too, but I find that these go best in terms of texture and flavour).
- Garlic—Slice the garlic into discs. Heat up the vegetable oil, once medium hot, add the garlic slices. Fry them till they are golden brown. Constantly monitor them while frying as garlic takes just a few seconds to burn. Remove from oil and drain on a paper napkin.
- Onions—Finely slice onions. Separate the layers. Use the same oil that you used for the garlic to fry them. They also need to be fried till golden brown. Again, you need to be vigilant because they can go from golden brown to burnt very quickly. Remove from oil, and drain on a paper napkin. They will seem soggy when you take them out of the pan, but they crisp up once the oil drains and they cool down. Fry the onions in batches of two or three to get an even browning.
- (Preparing these two toppings requires the most amount of patience through this recipe. And I believe that learning how to fry them is a serious skill given the amount of practice it has taken me to get it just right!)

2. Preparing the curry/noodles:

- Heat up oil in a vessel of choice. (You can either use 2 tbsp of the flavoured oil used to fry the garlic and onions, or fresh cooking oil.)
- To that add the cumin, whole red chillies and curry leaves. Sauté for a few seconds until aromatic, then

add the coconut milk. Alternately, you can use 400 ml coconut milk and 200 ml vegetable or chicken stock if you would like to thin down the consistency of the curry or dilute a bit of that coconut flavour.

- Add the coriander powder, turmeric powder and salt. Let it come to a boil. Your curry is ready!
- Along with the curry, you can simultaneously boil the noodles/ spaghetti according to package instructions. Once cooked, drain, rinse with room temperature water, drizzle olive oil on to them and toss by hand so they don't get stuck together.

3. Assembling the individual bowls at the table:

- Place the desired quantity of noodles in a bowl. Pour a generous ladle of the curry, enough to soak the noodles. Add the veggies, eggs followed by the fried onions, fried garlic, peanuts, green chillies and finish off with a squeeze of lime!
- You could also add chicken to the dish by separately cooking cubed boneless chicken breast marinated in salt, ginger-garlic paste and lime.

Food as Memory

Richa Sharma-Dhamorikar

'Ma, I don't want to cook, I will never cook. I will only eat what you prepare and be happy. Not everyone needs to know how to cook, Ma!' My mother had to hear this throughout my growing years. Like most of us, I took homemade food for granted. I would come home from school, college, or from another city and I knew Ma would always dish out delicious food to me. Oh, and I had excuses to *not* eat most of the greens and 'boring' dishes, daals or simple homemade subjis. I looked forward to weekends when we had a full South Indian feast, Ma whipping up amazing dosas, idlis, appams, stew, divine idiyappams (string hoppers) and also North Indian specials like paneer dishes, chole bhature, poori aloo. Needless to say, these were the dishes and days I looked forward to, completely ignoring the regular weekday meals.

Then I moved, first to Mumbai for my Master's and then to Pune for my first job. Mumbai meant living alone for the first time, away from the comfort of home, with the full freedom to eat whatever, drink whatever, sleep whenever, go wherever...And I did just that. I did not miss the home-cooked meals in the beginning. Whenever I went back home for vacations, Ma would call me ahead of time and ask me what all I wanted to eat during my stay. I always said 'paneer, chole, pav bhaji, pakodas, more paneer, dosa, idiyappam, puttu (steamed rice flour rolls)' and she ensured I would get my stomachful of yumminess. She never complained how much of a task it was to get all the groceries for all these different dishes, she never said a word on how much preparation went into making some of those items, she never expressed the exhaustion that she must have felt while cooking with her backaches and joint pains. Nothing, not a word.

When I moved to Pune, I longed to get a whiff of Ma's cooking. The first job and the first salaries meant going out more and becoming a part of the 'I-live-for-weekends-let's-eat-and-drink' phase and that is what I did at first. But then I started missing family and home food. I realised that the void of home-cooked food started getting bigger. So now when Ma called before my trips home, I listed my favourites but also told her I would eat whatever she cooked. Tinda, tori, lauki, karela, sitaphal and I honestly meant it. Living away from home made me realise the importance of having home-cooked food, of having your mother or father lovingly ask you if you had had food/snacks/tea as they did that over the phone as well, of having fights with my brother over who would get what, of conversations around the table, eating together, discussing all things: life, politics, family, jokes. I only realised and longed for this once I didn't have it any longer.

Before I got married, I moved back home for a year because I wanted to spend time with my family. That whole year, I relished every meal that was set out for me—without a complaint, without a tantrum, without an excuse. In 2017, I got married, left home and family, moved to a new place, a new home and began a new phase of life. I remember Ma came down and stayed with us for a few days and helped me to get the kitchen essentials. I tried to cook every meal in the beginning as I had time and I wanted to cook my food my way. And in the beginning, I was slow, taking hours to make simple daal-chawal, which my husband still teases me about. I worked in the kitchen thinking and wondering how our mothers cooked for a family of four to five people without fail every single day, every single meal. It was beyond my comprehension. Getting married was no feat at all mainly because I had married the love of my life but settling down and making it on my own in a new city among new faces was definitely nerve-wracking. Oftentimes I wondered how to go about grocery shopping, listing stuff I needed, but there was never enough food or space in the kitchen. I feared I was not moving enough, or doing enough, and instead of making home-cooked meals, I started relying on food delivery apps.

I have always believed in 'to hell with what people say, I'll follow my heart' but somehow, somewhere the pressures of being a new wife, of having my own kitchen and meals to take care of, started getting to me. The anxiety affected my sleep, a phase of job-hunting made it worse, and I had terrible mood swings, days of feeling just 'down and out' and started preparing daal-chawal almost every second day without enjoying the process. At that time, Ma told me that dinner is probably the only time both of you get to eat meals together so just try to make an effort, if possible, and you will be fine. And that is what I did. I started calling Ma for her recipes and she told me the tiny tips that made my dishes amazing like hers. Of course, I could never ever be at par with her, but a bowl of ghee daal, brown rice and papadam gave me the familiar feeling of being home.

Throughout my life, two things always distinctly remind me of home: news channels constantly running in the background and the aroma of delicious homemade food. I could easily access news channels but I also started to turn towards cooking as my solace, of feeling closer to home, of having my family around me. Every time I added crushed garlic pods to ghee for tempering of daal, or curry leaves from my garden to the upma, I was reminded of home. It is strange how aromas evoke strong connections, taking you to places and people.

With Ma's and my husband's encouragement, I tried to make sambhar-dosa and pav-bhaji. That hot piping bowl of sambhar felt like a hug in a cup. That was my comfort food. The butter melting on the hot bhaji gave me a jolt of happiness because I knew I was just one bowl away from being home. Cooking gave me that sense of familiarity which I so needed in a new city, among new people, and in new situations. It helped me as a therapy to cope with the anxiety that comes with setting up new homes and new lives.

I am a much better, much sorted, much practiced cook now. I don't cook every day, and I still can't get over how Ma did that all those years. But I love trying out new recipes with and without success. I even baked my very first cake last year. I read cookbooks, the ones which have stories and recipes. I like plating my dishes, I like tweaking existing recipes, I try making salads more colourful, more tempting and I've started venturing into Maharashtrian cuisine. My husband is Maharashtrian and I never got to know or meet my mother-in-law to get tips, tricks and recipes from her so I try in my own ways. There are still times when I call up Ma and ask her to repeat a recipe because I have not noted it down. Every time I call, Ma says 'This is the last time I am telling you, not again' and yet she always does.

To all the mothers who cook for their children and families, day and night, on holidays, on weekends, handling the office and chores alongside, and pour all their love and warmth into those dishes, you truly are and will always be our stars! There can never be anyone like you and I wish, pray, hope to be even a small bit of what my Ma is. And yes, to all the fathers who help out and support mothers in the kitchen, or during grocery shopping, or sometimes even take over the kitchens. This story is for all of you.

Recipe: Richa's Ma's Sambhar

Ingredients:

For cooking daal:

1 cup toor daal (pigeon pea)
2.5 cups water (*Tip: Measure the water according to the second mark on your index finger—any hand—very Ma style)*
½ tsp turmeric
½ tsp salt
A pinch /¼ tsp asafoetida (hing)

For tamarind mix:

1 small ball tamarind
[*Tip: Squeeze a tiny ball of tamarind in your fist; it should be the size of a small lemon/amla (gooseberry)*]
Half cup water

For the veggie mix:

2 or 3 tomatoes (2 if you want the yumminess; 3 if you want it tangier!)—cut roughly into pieces

1 drumstick, cut into long pieces, each about 3-4 inches
5 or 6 shallots cut roughly into pieces (two regular onions
    if you can't find shallots but Ma says shallots take the
    dish to another level altogether and I couldn't agree
    more!)
1 carrot (any variety will do, orange/red) cut into long
    pieces
4 or 5 beans cut into long pieces
2 tbsp roughly chopped coriander
For the sambhar masala:
1 tbsp coriander powder
1 tbsp red chilli powder
4 or 5 methi (fenugreek) seeds (More than this will make
    the sambhar very bitter)

For the tempering:

1 tbsp coconut oil
1 tsp mustard seeds
1 sprig or 4-5 curry leaves
¼ onion or 2 shallots, finely chopped
1 pinch of red chilli powder

Method:

1. Cooking daal:

- Wash the toor daal in water till it runs clean. Put in a
  pressure cooker with water (as specified above).
- Add the cut tomatoes, beans, carrots and onions. (If not
  using shallots, put onions in this step.)
- Let it cook for 4 to 5 whistles. Let the pressure settle
  down on its own. Open the lid and let it sit.

2. Preparing the tamarind water:

- Soak the tamarind ball in water.
- Set it aside for 15 minutes (minimum) or 25 (maximum).
- Once done, squeeze the tamarind ball in the soaked water to get as much juice as possible.
- Keep this water aside.

3. Cooking shallots and drumsticks:

- In a small pan, put in one drumstick (cut into 3-4 inch pieces) and shallots with water.
- Add a pinch of turmeric.
- Cook on a low flame for 8-10 minutes.
- The drumstick should be a little soft and pulpy. You should be able to insert a fork in it smoothly.
- Once they are done, drain the water and set them aside.

4. Making the sambhar masala:

- Take a small iron pan (the ones used in Indian kitchens for *tadka*).
- On a low flame, dry roast the methi seeds first (not more than 4-5). They will start turning a little brown and start to pop.
- To the same pan add 1 tbsp coriander powder and dry roast it. When it starts getting darker it is roasted enough.
- Then add 1 tbsp red chilli powder and dry roast it as well.
- Let this mix cool off a bit. Be warned that dry roasting these spices gives off a very strong aroma!
- Keep this aside.

5. Making the magic paste:

- Put the dry roasted spices in a mixer-grinder.
- Take half cup of the tamarind water and add it to the mixer. (You can also put in more if you want a stronger tamarind tang.)
- Grind it into a fine paste. (It will be a shiny, brown paste.)

6. Putting them together:

- Put the pressure cooker with the cooked daal and veggies on the stove and let it come to a boil on a low flame.
- Add the boiled shallots and drumsticks to the sambhar.
- Then add the magic paste to the sambhar and stir well.
- The sambhar will start looking brown in colour. Let it boil for a few minutes.
- Add 1 tbsp of fresh coriander and stir well.
- Add any remaining tamarind water to the cooker and stir.

7. Time for the tempering:

- In a small pan (iron pan or any that you have) heat 1 tbsp of coconut oil.
- Add 1 tsp mustard seeds and let them splutter.
- Add a pinch of asafoetida.
- Add curry leaves (4-5).
- Add half of a small onion (or 2 shallots).
- Let it cook for a minute.
- Switch off the flame.
- Add a pinch of red chilli powder on top of this mix. Mix it with a spoon. (It is important to switch off the flame before adding the red chilli powder as otherwise it tends to get burnt a bit).

- Add to the sambhar and stir well.
- Garnish with loads of fresh, finely cut coriander and relish a piping hot bowl of one type of Kerala-style sambhar!

Please note you can tweak the quantity of the ingredients depending on your taste preferences. It will still be yummy!

The Making of Food

A Daily Riyaaz towards the Music of True Healing

Lina Krishnan

In my childhood, there was one place that was absolutely fun to visit. This was my aunt's farm in Kerala. As Delhi children, we gladly exchanged the dusty desert for the verdant landscape of palm trees and mango orchards. At the time, there was no direct road to get to the farm, and no electricity there. The motorable road stopped at the edge of the paddy fields and to reach the homestead, you had to walk on a narrow mud path with water on both sides. One wrong move and you could be in waist-deep water with the rice and the snakes. It made for quite an exciting journey and even before we reached, my aunt and her family would be up on the hillock encouraging us with waves of welcome. Cousins to swim with in the pond, the cows to greet by name, pallanguzhi (a board game we played in the evening), a twinkling uncle telling us rambling stories by lamplight. Oh, why did we ever grow up?

My parents seemed younger and happier in these surroundings as well. Athai—my father's sister—was endearing because she was perennially cheerful and relaxed unlike my burdened parents who would quickly bolt their food down before rushing to work. Perhaps it had something to do with being rooted in her environment, no commute or job stress, and being completely one with nature. Have we lost that relationship with food nowadays? The kitchen is no longer central to our lives; work predominates and we just grab the odd bite and carry on. Cooking too has become a solitary activity, except for the occasional party. Perhaps it's because we are also disconnected to other aspects of food. Today, much of its growing happens far away, the materials often arrive at the door, or cooking itself is outsourced.

In contrast, everything that Athai cooked came from the farm. If it was summer, then we would be in the midst of the chakka-manga season, as the jackfruit and mango were called. The orchard behind the house would be brimming with both, and we would go with a butterfly net to tip the mangoes in. Jackfruit was a tougher proposition, but there was gentle smiling Neli, my aunt's farmhand. She would divest the fruit of its crinkly exterior, expertly extract the over-sweet fruit, which I hated, and finally work out an elaborate process to make the delicious jam. One spoon and you would be in heaven.

Then would begin the making of that rare treat, which we could never get anywhere else: elai adai, a sweet pancake steamed in banana leaf. This was, typically, a group activity. To the freshly made jackfruit jam made by Neli, my aunt would add a vast amount of grated coconut. The thick syrupy mixture was then kept aside. My mother would gather banana leaves, and wash and then dry them by lightly holding them close to a wood fire. On those leaves would go circles of rice paste, and the jam-coconut mix would be spread on this base. Then the rice paste circle would be folded in half and put into the steamer. One steamer could take up to twenty at a time. And it needed to, given the number of folks waiting eagerly to sample these delightful goodies.

The homestead is long gone, the children scattered across the world. And I have to buy the jam now, in season. But just a spoonful even now transports me to that smoky kitchen with its rafters hanging with plantains, the deep well of sweet water outside, and the sense of enjoyment imbued in its very pores.

Food is like that. A particular taste, or fragrance or sight is enough to bring back things and people we thought we had forgotten. When I stir a stew, I think of the varied flavours my friends can create for the same dish, the jars of gujia (a sweet of stuffed coconut and sugar), tengoyal (a fried rice-daal snack) and special tamarind stews that my mother still sometimes pampers us with, and her sister's inordinate love for that most basic of comfort foods, tairchaadam aka dahi chawal or dahi bhaat. I recall my oldest aunt's special book, filled with a hundred recipes, written painstakingly by hand over seventy years, copies of which are now shared sparingly with select sisters-in-law and nieces. The comfort zone of memories is healing.

The other day, I was making rotis, and alongside, drawing my usual pictures in the flour dust. Something about the rough texture of the ragi (finger millet) and the fragrance of the roti makes me dreamy. And it made me recall Paati, my mother's mother. She taught me how to make rotis when I was twelve. And she in turn, had encountered Punjabi neighbours and learnt these unfamiliar northern dishes over the garden wall, as it were.

My parents, to whom kids were made for studies and more studies, never encouraged us to do anything around the house. Paati in contrast, believed that using one's hands and being self-reliant were more reliable tools in the journey of life. She herself was an epitome of these values that had steered her from young widowhood to a resilient middle age, at which she embarked on a new adventure, arriving in Delhi, with her sturdy face and her colourful nine-yard sarees, to create a bulwark for her then-unmarried young daughters. Whether they faced harassment at work, or difficulties while doing their PhD, they had a home to return to, where their mother's common sense, firm principles and comforting food would shore them up for another day in the new milieu.

I mention her here because kitchens and gardens were her keys to staying buoyant through assorted changes. She had incredible green thumbs. Oh, the flowers she could and did grow! When I think of her, something of her spirit comes through to me, in me. As a fifty-plus Tamilian in Delhi, barely knowing Hindi, how did she find her way around a city that is not particularly kind or helpful to outsiders? Her resourcefulness in these new surroundings was remarkable. She went everywhere, and got to know everything, on her own. My other grandmother, in contrast, never stepped out, but she had a fund of wild Tamil stories, and sang her way through cooking, something I do as well, except that she sang much better!

When I stir a spinach curry now, I remember her teasing me for my limited repertoire as a new bride. In those days, this was the only 'proper' dish I knew and I made it frequently. I had no idea then that it was also healthy. And even to this limited cooking I had arrived quite late.

When you're young and immersed in work and partying, words like healthy eating or traditional cuisine mean very little. When I left home, the heady sense of the new life was so liberating that the old one gracefully took a backseat. It was only one night when I was eating my fourth bowl of heated-over rajma and realised how many pizzas I had downed from sheer inertia, that I sensed a certain lack of well-being.

Was it the spices and flavours, not to mention the incredible lightness of being, of my mom's curries and my dad's fruit salads? Sure, I missed my folks, but I never thought about the two decades of delectable food I had taken for granted. Far from it, I used to call it boring and wish I could be a *bon vivant*. And now, without warning, that same old boring home food had sneaked up on me and I was longing for it. This is not to say that the advantages of cooking one's food, or the creativity that's an intangible part of the process, dawned on me like an epiphany. It has taken over twenty years of daily cooking in all weathers and locales. At times, it does seem like a slog, but to be able to eat just what your taste buds crave is worth the work.

It's like riyaaz, the daily practice of musical notes, without which there would be no true music.

In fact, many gurus have spoken of the close connection between music and cooking. Vocalist extraordinaire Ustad Bade Ghulam Ali Khan would cook up enormous feasts before his concerts, while Ustad Bismillah Khan, magician with the shehnai, would tell his students to sing the ragas they were learning while cooking or washing clothes, make it a part of everyday life and not a rarefied object.

As for me, I find that, in cooking, the jingle-jangles of problems elsewhere often find resolution here. In this summer of discontent, the only thing keeping me sane, besides my poetry, is cooking. There are days when the words won't ring true, but even then the next meal has to be made. When I pare the amaranth leaves or sort the daals that will go into the idli mix, or sit down with a cup of adrak (ginger) chai, I can almost forget the problems afflicting our world. It makes one remember the essential truths that will be true no matter what's in store for us; nature doesn't change, and the folks who really matter to us, hopefully will not, either.

RECIPE: PARIKYA PITLA (BITTER GOURD CURRY)

In terms of specifics, the food we eat every day is what you could call typical Tamil Brahmin vegetarian food, with a distinct touch of Kerala. It's light and cooling, as the region's intense heat needs. The spices vary from red to green chillies, jeera to mustard, use daal or don't, use coconut or don't, and every meal calls for a vegetable or even four, stir-fried or immersed in curd or in a curry. In short, there's a whole world out there and it's all vegetarian, fresh, yummy and reasonably low on oil, unlike a lot of other Indian cooking. I think only Assamese food could be described as lighter. Parikya pitla is a favourite with my Punjabi mate and in-laws, and we end up having it about once a fortnight. In turn, he treats me to his version of Arya Samaji Punjabi food (austere but delicious). So one of our two meals is Carnatic, and the other Hindustani, so to speak. As in music and food, so in life—the more diverse, the better our universe!

Like many secret sauces, the pitla recipe I have included here is principally a home dish; you will never find it in a restaurant. It's fairly simple to make.

This dish is best served with plain rice; it goes well with papadams and/or a simple side dish of pumpkin.

Serves 3

Ingredients:

3 bitter gourds (karela/parikya), medium-sized, de-
    skinned and diced into cubes
1 large scoop arhar daal
Tamarind, a lemon-sized ball
1 tbsp urad/toor daal (split pigeon pea lentil)
Quarter of a small coconut
1 or 2 red chillies, according to taste
1 tsp jaggery powder
Asafoetida (hing), a pinch
Salt to taste
Karipatta (a single curry leaf does wonders to the taste)
¼ tsp mustard seeds
Ghee for tadka (tempering)

Method:

- Wash the arhar daal thoroughly. Soak in water for about 30 minutes. Cook with a little water and salt till well done. Mash.
- Soak the tamarind in a bit of water for 10 minutes and squeeze it out or strain it. Add a pinch of asafoetida to the tamarind water. Add the vegetable cubes and boil until done. Leave aside.
- Stir fry the urad daal till it turns golden. Add the red chilli and switch off the flame. Once it cools, grind the piece of coconut and then add the chilli-daal mix and grind that. Add to the cooked vegetable.
- Now add the previously well-cooked arhar daal to this mix and stir briefly on a very low flame, as daal is apt to catch at the bottom. Once you see bubbles forming, it is done.

- Put aside. Add the spoonful of jaggery powder. This offsets the bitterness of the gourd and improves taste all around.
- The final tempering: In a tadka scoop, heat a half spoon of ghee. If you don't have ghee, any cooking oil will do. To this add a tiny portion of mustard seeds and once it sputters, switch off and add a curry leaf. Add this to the dish.

Voila! Enjoy your pitla.

Tryst with Tea

Pooja Priyamvada

'*A cup of tea would restore my normality.*'

—*Hitchhiker's Guide to the Galaxy*,
screenplay, Douglas Adams

I have unique Punjabi and Pahari genes in equal measure and yet could never become somebody who can be called a real foodie. An experimentalist for sure, I try new things and relish them too. But in day-to-day living, I can eat the same boring home breakfast for decades and be content. One of the reasons for sticking to limited choices could also be my physical and mental illnesses that happened early in childhood.

I was always a sickly child and was afflicted with weird things like goitre, styes in my eyelids and a myriad other ailments. This was in spite of all the vaccinations, diet and extra care I received, being the only child of my parents. As I look back, I realise I also had some eating disorder during my teenage years, maybe due to my weight issues and some other psychological issues.

My first tryst with depression was when I was barely fourteen and just a few months before my tenth class board exams. On the day of my first internal exam, I woke up and couldn't stand on my feet. I was rushed to the hospital in a state of panic by my late father. Even amidst that chaos, he remembered to carry one thing—a flask of tea for both of us.

By evening, I found myself in a wheelchair due to what was believed to be a severe bone infection. It was misdiagnosed as tuberculosis and I was bedridden for several weeks with a brick traction on my left leg. The bad mental health following that was attributed to post-traumatic stress disorder (PTSD) and pressures of the boards. Although my father was supportive as ever and even wanted me to skip that year, the year went by in a blur.

During those bedridden months, a new relationship blossomed in my life—a lifelong relationship with tea and writing. I struggled with mental health and osteoid osteoma in the successive years. But as they say, for every ailment of the mind or body, there is a tea!

In my college years, I went through the normal curve of experimentation both personally and socially, had relationships, new passions like theatre and art. Through all of this, I remained a tea-lover. When I moved to the plains from Shimla, where tea was less popular in homes and hostels, and when there were bad bouts of physical and mental illness, I still found solace in my 'childhood love'.

Any kind of mental health challenge, of course, has its scientific and medical progression, symptoms and remedies, but what is peculiar is how each survivor also subjectively processes it. So what they find solace and strength from is also varied, and often sadly when the comfort comes from food, it results into 'comfort eating', which in itself is a disorder of sorts.

In my case as well, I indulged in a lot of unhealthy comfort eating during bad bouts of anxiety and depression. It affected my physical health badly. During postpartum depression, after my daughter was born, I was suicidal. I was so sick that I would think about foods that could kill.

During these years besides parenthood, the only other good thing that happened to me was lots of travel. I tried new cuisines, new kinds of teas and my repertoire in the culinary skills section also expanded. Soon my child was weaned to solid food. For the first time in my life, I started experimenting with recipes and enjoying their outcomes. Finally I started eating healthy and enjoyed the positive effects it had on my overall health and wellbeing.

And then came fibromyalgia with a severity of symptoms. I lost a lot of grip in my fingers and was unable to even hold a spoon or a cup. Cooking had to be curtailed because I would often get cuts, bruises and burns. But my love for tea, which had always been therapeutic, continued with a wide variety of teas from the world over. With that, I started managing symptoms like brain fog and sleep issues better.

The illnesses remain. The strains of work and single parenting remain. My cup of tea remains my solace in every storm. I often resort to a strong cup of black tea when I have a professional deadline to meet. I have a mild jasmine tea on balmy afternoons. Fruit teas, hot and cold, are best for evenings and Afghani tea with honey or maybe chamomile at night. But in between all these, there is something that always works for me, my personalised version of the Indian chai, that I believe has a hint of how my father used to make it in Shimla winters, in a Railway style ketli (calling it a kettle would be blasphemy!). The best part now is that sometimes my offspring also enjoys a sip and I get compliments for making the best chai in this world.

Recipe: Masala Chai

Here is my recipe for basic Indian masala chai that I often drink. This is usually my first cuppa as well as the sunset cuppa, drunk alone for the last many years now. This never fails me whether I need solace, warmth or just the feeling of having something valuable to hold on to.

Serves 1 cup

Ingredients:

1.5 teacups water
4 pods green cardamom
2 tsp sugar (optional)
1 inch long thin slice ginger (optional)
3 tsp tea (any good brand; 3 tsp is what I prefer but can
    be adjusted according to taste)
Half a cup of milk

Method:

- Mix the water and milk in a pan and put on medium flame.
- Crush the cardamom pods and add to the mix along with the ginger (if using), and bring to a boil.
- Add the tea, lower the flame, cover and let simmer for about 2 minutes.
- Add sugar if using.
- Sieve into your favourite mug and serve hot.

Baking, Curiosity and Learning to Live with My Mental Disorder

Divya Kandwal

It was the second time when I landed in a hospital, and then a psychiatrist's office, that I realised that my mental disorder would most certainly kill me. For years prior to this incident, I had thought of my intrusive thoughts, anxiety and depression as facets of my mind that crippled and incapacitated me but also made me who I was. But at twenty-one, I was completely sure that this would be the end of me.

My first memory of a panic attack goes back to when I was nine and stopped eating, talking and doing my class work. The memory is hazy, as if I'm looking back through a cracked, stained-glass window but I have my journals and the feeling of something being scooped out of my chest to go back to.

Reading and writing had always been sources of comfort and respite for me. Which is why it was increasingly distressing to me when I lost the ability to do both. I have tried and failed to write this essay several times. Every time I sit down and start, my mind goes blank and I feel this heaviness in my head, as if all my thoughts are merely white noise.

This is in part, what led me to the office of a condescending psychiatrist right after my twenty-second birthday. Out of all the rubbish suggestions he gave me, one stuck. Baking.

But I don't think he should get the credit for it. He suggested that I try to find joy in activities that I used to previously delight in. This is extremely bad advice. Depression robs you of the ability to experience happiness or pleasure. It robs you of the ability to feel. In India, people expect those who suffer from mental disorders to walk around with shaggy hair and rumpled clothes. Sometimes, I was able to dress up, leave my house and attend classes and was therefore thought of as indulgent, lazy, and dramatic. I was thought of as someone who was merely pretending to be ill for attention and pity. What people don't realise is that we dress up and put on a face as a desperate attempt to hold on to the last shred of our sanity, to at least appear normal. Which is why, I took my psychiatrist's bad advice and tried to bake once again.

And it changed my life.

I wish that were true. It did not.

The last time I had baked anything was almost four years ago, back in high school. In college, I turned vegan in a desperate attempt to cure myself. It didn't help of course. Contrary to popular belief, one cannot simply will their mental illness away. But rediscovering baking led me to a very important realisation which is—all my previous recipes were useless as they contained some form of egg or dairy. Most of my attempts resulted in things that were inedible. I still don't know why but I continued. Giving up comes as easily to me as mumbling my words. Maybe it was the obsessive part of my mind taking over or maybe I was desperate to prove to myself that I could create something. But whatever it was, it gave me curiosity about the future. Not hope, not excitement but a tiny speck of curiosity. And it was enough. Vegan baking was a long ordeal of trial and failure. It resulted in days spent crying in bed and angry shattering of bowls against the floor. But it also gave me a reason to get out of bed, go to the shops and try again.

Usually, I ordered all the ingredients I needed online. But as baking changed from something I did to fill the gaps in my day, something to break the monotony of mostly lying in bed to something I sometimes enjoyed, I started getting restless. The restlessness and as I now realise, maybe excitement encouraged me to venture outside.

The physical act of measuring, stirring, and kneading somehow quieted my mind. It wasn't a miracle. Struggling with mental illness does not leave much space for hope or miracles. But baking gave me a routine. It became and still is my way of meditating, of practicing mindfulness. Somehow along the way, my perspective on baking shifted. It became less about the result and getting everything right, and more about the process itself. Anxiety is a thief of life. It renders a person completely incapable of living in the moment. Baking gave me the space to try and experience the present, while still managing my anxiety about the future.

For me, the process goes like this. I collect all the ingredients, prep the oven, and start. I lay out everything I need on the kitchen counter and double-check the ingredients on my list. Focusing on the physical aspect of food, on how it feels in my hands, its texture, and consistency inadvertently taught me how to manage my intrusive thoughts. It grounded me in reality. It tied me to actuality. It taught me how to ignore my intrusive thoughts and that it was okay when I couldn't. Just like cooking and baking, healing is also a process. Food is fuel, it is energy, and yet it is also temporary. You consume it and it's gone. Healing, like baking, is a practice.

So over time, baking became something akin to therapy for me.

Substituting eggs and dairy for plant-based ingredients showed me that nothing, NOTHING is indispensable. It was staggering to realise that you could replace any ingredient in a recipe and it would still turn out to be all right, if not perfect.

This transformed how I viewed my mental disorder. It was mind-blowing to discover that like a recipe, I do not need to possess qualities that people consider important to validate my existence. Living in a capitalist society, our personal worth is intricately netted with our economic value. Mental disorders are incapacitating and paralysing, which induces a lot of shame and guilt.

A friend once told me that it is all right to not be hopeful about the future. It is enough if all you feel is a bit of curiosity about how your life is going to play out. Baking taught me that even though my mental illness robbed me of qualities that might have made me a productive member of society, it was okay. I would lead a small, quiet life. But a small life can be satisfying too. After all, courage doesn't always have to be loud.

Recipe: Vegan, Double Chocolate Banana Muffins

This recipe yields 10 muffins.

Ingredients:

Dry Ingredients

1½ cups all-purpose flour
½ cup oats
½ cup brown sugar
1 tbsp baking powder
½ tbsp baking soda
½ tbsp vanilla powder
4 tbsp cocoa powder
1 cup dark chocolate chunks
A pinch of salt
Wet Ingredients
2 ripe, mashed bananas
¼ cup coconut oil
½ cup plant milk
1 chia egg*
4 tbsp vegan yoghurt (optional)

Method:

- Preheat the oven to 180°C/350⁰ F .
- In a large mixing bowl, mix all the dry ingredients. In a separate bowl, mix the wet ingredients. Combine the dry and wet ingredients.
- Line a muffin tray with liners and fill them about three-fourth leaving a bit of space at the top.
- Bake for 15 to 16 minutes.
- Insert a toothpick in a muffin. If it comes out clean, the muffins are done.

- Mix 1 tablespoon of chia seeds with 3 tablespoons of water. Keep aside for 10 minutes. If you don't have chia seeds, ground flax seeds will work just as well.

Food for Thought

Payal Kapoor

My earliest memories of recognising that food was more than just what went into the mouth to be savoured, was when I was still a little girl. Watching my restauranteur uncle cut, chop and toss a bunch of vegetables, meats, oils and spices etc. around with a magician's flourish, turning it all into something deliciously edible, had me transfixed and involuntarily mirroring his moves with my empty, little girl hands. I didn't ever think this would translate into anything more than a passing interest or momentary fascination. However, the interest didn't wane; it only morphed into a fixation with vegetables and fruits in particular. Why that was, I'll never be sure. Perhaps it was the visual delight and appeal of the various shapes, colours and textures of nature's bounty that called to me.

My visits to the traditional vegetable and fruit market were a visual and olfactory delight. Everything was stacked high in baskets, looking so pretty and tempting that resisting the urge to reach out and touch was almost impossible. The shiny and colourful palate of the wares still stays a vivid memory, years after I became blind—reds of tomatoes, greens of varied leafy vegetables, shades of purple of brinjals...I could go on and on. The 'Bhaiya' always obliged with a taste of the juiciest tomatoes and raw mangoes when in season. The quick and efficient slices made with their sharp knives were a treat to watch.

So, when years later I found myself enrolling in a three-year course in hotel management, nobody was surprised. Right from the word go, I knew I would become a chef at the end of the three years and work my magic in the kitchen—cutting, chopping, whipping and cooking up a storm. The three years were a revelation of the best kind. From learning the right way to use the various tools and gadgets in a commercial kitchen, to the various kinds of cooking methods to delving into the history and cuisines of countries far and wide—a culinary journey in the truest sense of the word.

Then there was the introduction to the world of raw materials, and all the fascinating ingredients that made for a learning experience for life. How a collection of powders, flours and a little bit of this and that translated into an aromatic plateful of good food left me more convinced where my career path lay.

But then, who ever said life went according to plan? In the course of my three years in college, many decisions changed and I ended up not being a chef after all. However, my love for food and dabbling in it at home didn't change. I was the gourmet food expert at home who went out and hunted strange ingredients and made new things for all at home. No regular food for me...after all I was a chef wannabe, wasn't I?

Then, a few years down the line, catastrophe struck, spiralling my life out of orbit—never to be the same again. This marked the second phase...as I live it today.

I was twenty-two when an unexplained and then

undiagnosed cerebral attack struck and damaged most of my sensory system. In a matter of weeks, I was reduced from being a healthy, happy young girl to a diminished disabled person—physically, mentally and emotionally.

The attack left me totally blind, hearing-impaired, and with no sense of taste or smell. My sense of touch was left patchy too. Any dreams or aspirations I'd ever had for my life were gone forever. Left debilitated, I never thought I would ever again do any of the things I'd so loved. There must have been some method to the universe's madness to have had me record so many visual and olfactory memories in all the years when I took delight in absorbing them. Staying imprinted in my brain, they served to be the perfect images to recall in a flashback when life did indeed move on, as unbelievable as it may have seemed at the time.

It took me two hospital stints and many months of alternative therapy to finally realise my disability was irreversible and I would be deaf-blind forever. It was a shock to say the least and as I saw the last of the hope drain out of my life, true devastation set in. How was I going to live the rest of my life? Closed in an emotional hell, I fell into a deep depression and an abyss of hopelessness. Barely able to lift my hands to feel anything, there was no way I'd return to the kitchen and my experiments there. I could not taste anything I ate, or smell what went into my mouth. My family had devised a method of writing on my palm using their fingers to communicate with me. That was the extent of my knowledge of what I ate. For someone who loved food and the smells and colours of food, this was a deathly blow. How much more was going to be taken away from me—I was afraid to even think about it.

Fortunately for me, with the help of alternative

treatments and medication, my sense of smell and taste began to revive. It was a strange experience to be able to smell and taste, but with a twist; it felt slightly different from the way it should be. Underdeveloped for a long time, I often found myself guessing things wrong. It did eventually become completely normal and I went from having an underdeveloped sense to a hyper-sensitive one—something I am eternally grateful for.

Gradually my hearing returned as well. From being a soft, far away sound, to a garbled and then clear one (although only in my right ear), I was elated to be able to hear again. I almost didn't believe it when I first heard the sound of a crow from very far away in my right ear. After that, I strained to absorb everything that was a sound to assure myself that I was indeed hearing again. From here on, things began looking up again. My sense of touch was still patchy, but I could now lift my hands and feel things I touched. It was not the best but I'd learned to be grateful for the small steps towards near-normalcy my life was taking.

Once the dust had settled after all the upheaval my life had been put through, I returned home. Everything was new and different—of course it was, I was seeing nothing and hearing very little. My mother, the superwoman, decided enough time had been wasted in trying to revive a physical condition which may never change. She believed if it had to, it would on its own, and waiting for it was a fruitless task.

So off she went, thinking of all the things I could do around the house. Devising things and thinking up all she would herself do without consciously seeing. Among the first tasks was handling vegetables. After all, who needed to see to string beans or grate carrots? I distinctly remember the feeling of putting my hands into a bowl of cold French beans and feel tears well up in my eyes. It had been so long since I had felt anything clearly enough using my hands. I had always loved cutting and chopping vegetables; but this was far beyond anything I had felt before. This time I was actually concentrating on the texture, shape and structure of the vegetable, which so far had been a mechanical task.

I could smell the vegetable when it was first peeled and then cut. Everything I had thought of as lost came rushing back in that one moment. It was exhilarating! It was as natural as doing it every day for all of my life. My loss of sight or the dimming of other senses had been relegated completely to a corner at the back of my mind, never to surface again.

Since I could use a knife without using the chopping board, cutting came easy. Slowly, deliberately at first, and then with increasing confidence, I remember the first batch of beans and carrots I'd chopped. Running my hands through it gave me a sense of accomplishment like none other. It grounded me in some weird way. I loved the order and symmetry of the shapes and enjoyed the precision of the task. This beginning was nearly thirty-one years back and my love for reducing mounds of vegetables into various shapes and sizes has stayed with me.

It made me feel like I was contributing in some way at home and that small boost of encouragement went a long way in bolstering my sense of self-worth. This became a cathartic sort of a routine during the later years when I was struggling in my marriage as well.

I still remember the first time my instructor, a blind man himself, initiated me to light the gas stove all on my own, drizzle oil into a kadhai or wok and put into it okra that I had chopped myself. My mother, mortally afraid I would burn myself and the house down, walked out of the kitchen. It didn't stop me from going through the motions, burning my fingers a time or two, but in the end, completing the task assigned—cooking the vegetable to near-perfection.

That was a beginning of the revival of my love story with cooking once again. Each time I felt restless and needed a validation, cooking was always my go-to activity. It always did the much-needed picking up of my sense of self, cheered me up and gave the family something new to eat.

Soon, the degree of difficulty in what and how I cooked decreased and I found myself looking forward to experimenting with new ingredients and methods of cooking. Going from someone who couldn't smell and taste for a while, I went to being able to smell the degree of doneness of frying onions and could tell when the gravy was ready to pull off of the fire. Reading up recipes in Braille from any accessible source became a hobby and swapping ideas with friends on various new things became a catharsis.

I became more confident each time I pulled off cooking something that I'd never tried before without incident. Soon I was running my own home and kitchen confidently. At times when my marriage put me through the wringer, I found myself turning to a space within myself that was my safe space. Pulling all the raw vegetables out of the refrigerator, I'd start processing them to be used later— chopping, slicing/dicing, puréeing, etc. This single-minded concentration kept me from confrontations and gave me time to think and gather myself.

There were times when my ex-husband would not talk with me or eat the food I'd cooked as a way to punish me which he knew was something that bothered me the most.

I'd still cook and freeze food for the day he would come around. These were times when I kept myself grounded by simply churning out dish after dish.

It was when I started baking once again that I found my true joy. Always a little complicated, since the ingredients had to be in the exact measure, I'd never attempted baking after losing my sight. I discovered there were Braille labelled measuring cups and spoons, and realised I could mark my oven to identify temperature and modes that would make me independent. A talking weighing scale gave me precise measurements as well. I still remember going through the motions to bake my first cake—a hot milk sponge. The aroma of a baking cake was a high like none other. Being able to now make sweet treats on request and as gifts was humbling as it was uplifting. Each subsequent activity in the kitchen which I was able to perform independently was a step towards a new me.

Graduating to new and complex recipes to bake is a personal challenge I periodically put myself through. Each cake or dessert that I didn't get right would either deter me from trying it at all or go after it with gusto and keep at it until I got it right. In the community of blind persons, I soon found myself becoming a go-to person to learn cooking from. This was also a bolstering vote of confidence. The relevance of relationships forged in this process was more precious than I could have ever imagined. For every instance that I felt defeated and down, one call from someone looking for help in the kitchen lifted my spirit and made me believe in myself again. After all, when so many thought I was more than I believed I was, I must be...

Soon I found myself mentoring and teaching cooking and baking either in real-time or over the phone. I have walked friends through an entire evening of their cooking—guiding them every step of the way until they were done. All this with me over the phone as they cooked in their kitchens. Anyone who overheard thought we were crazy, but that sense of accomplishment on both sides was something only we could understand and relate to. The joy they felt at having served something to friends and family they'd cooked themselves and I having seen them through the entire process brought unparalleled satisfaction and a growing sense of being bigger than my disability. I was definitely no longer defined by my blindness or hearing impairment. Life had flung me far into the deep and I had managed to swim against the tide and make it to the other side. Not diminished or changed, but a whole new person.

RECIPE: CHOCOLATE BANANA BREAD

This is my favourite recipe and I bake it often. It's my go-to comfort food, both for me and anyone I think needs comforting. Easy to put together, this only needs measured ingredients and simply mixing together. No long-drawn whipping or fluffing. Just a happy wild chunky batter, which, when baked has a personality of its very own.

Adapted from www.joyofbaking.com

Ingredients:

½ cup (55 gm) toasted walnuts or pecans, coarsely chopped
1¾ cups (230 gm) all-purpose flour
¼ cup (30 gm) unsweetened cocoa powder (Dutch
    processed or regular)
1 cup (200 gm) granulated white sugar
1 tsp baking powder
¼ tsp baking soda
¼ tsp salt

½ cup (85 gm) white, dark, or milk chocolate chips
2 large eggs, lightly beaten
½ cup (113 gm) unsalted butter, melted and cooled
3 ripe bananas (454 gm), mashed well (about 1½ cups)
1 tsp pure vanilla extract

Method:

- Preheat oven to 350°F (180°C) and place oven rack to middle position.
- Butter and flour (or spray with a non-stick vegetable/ flour spray) the bottom and sides of a 9 x 5 x 3 inch (23 x 13 x 8 cm) loaf pan.
- Place the nuts on a baking sheet and bake for about 8 to 10 minutes or until lightly toasted. Let cool and then chop coarsely.
- In a large bowl whisk together the flour, cocoa powder, sugar, baking powder, baking soda, and salt.
- In a medium-sized bowl combine the mashed bananas, eggs, melted butter, and vanilla.
- With a rubber spatula or wooden spoon, lightly fold the wet ingredients (banana mixture) into the dry ingredients until just combined and batter is thick and chunky.
- Fold in the nuts and chocolate chips.
- Scrape batter into prepared pan and sprinkle the top of the bread with coarse brown sugar (optional).
- Bake until bread has risen and a toothpick inserted in the centre comes out clean, about 55 to 65 minutes.
- Place on a wire rack to cool and then remove the bread from the pan.
- Serve warm or at room temperature. Can be covered and stored for a few days, or frozen for longer storage.

Cookies and Poems: A Story of Sweet Saviours

Georgina Marie Guardado

Pre-2017, I had been a poet for half of my life but had primarily done so in seclusion, hardly ever sharing my work with the world with the exception of occasional newspaper publications or social media postings. In late 2017, I had begun attending poetry readings and workshops in my community and sharing my work. This shift may have come from a burst of confidence after ending a decade-long relationship the year prior and reconnecting with myself after feeling confined to a toxic partnership for so long. I also had been living with my closest sister who always encouraged me to just 'do it, see what happens'.

When I started sharing my work with others, I received an unexpected and overwhelming amount of support by other writers and members of the community and soon began to receive invitations for additional readings, radio shows; and with the encouragement of friends and family, I even applied for the Poet Laureate title in my county (which I didn't quite get but was one of three finalists which in itself is quite something). I started attending workshops at a local art centre in which the theme was resilience and through building connection with others, I became quickly comfortable with the group environment and found myself writing more truthfully, deeply, and poetically as I immersed myself in my local literary community. I was finally living as a full-fledged poet.

When I wasn't awarded the title of Poet Laureate in my county, I still felt drawn to be involved in my community by implementing some of the ideas I had for furthering the engagement of poetry within my rural county of residence. One of my first solo projects was planning, organising, and hosting poetry readings at my local farmers' market. This started off with a small Tuesday afternoon reading at a park and would end with a larger Saturday afternoon reading, to take place outdoors at a local winery and feature ten readers including two poets laureate from both Lake and Napa counties. I was both excited and nervous to make this a successful reading but my sister, one of my biggest fans, encouraged and supported me so much. She had been ill for quite a long time, suffering from a number of serious medical conditions but she too was full of anticipation for this event and was determined to be there herself, even though at the time she could hardly walk.

Leading up to this event, she would laud my progress as a poet. Not so much that I was a poet, but that I had been growing at such a rate that I was sharing my true self with the world around me and encouraging the same in other writers. She was biased of course, being my sister, my best friend. But I always took her love and support to heart. She was the type of person who was always brutally honest, whether it was positive or negative because she embodied being honest so if I made her proud, I was happy.

One July afternoon, after she was admitted to a nursing home after a long stay at a hospital, one of many unfortunate stays, we decided to go spend some time sitting outside in the courtyard of the nursing home so she could get some warmth from the sun and heat in her bones. We watched birds, looked at flowers and talked about how she'd be coming to my poetry reading. We talked about many things that day, about life, about simple things. She enjoyed the coffee I brought her and to finally have some fresh air beneath the sun after so many days and nights confined to hospital rooms. Then the unexpected happened. Just a few days after sitting in the sun together, she suddenly and unexpectedly passed away; my world didn't just turn upside town, it fell apart.

My sister was the one person in my life I was closest to. She was my sister, my best friend, and sometimes she was even my second mother. She was the one person in my life I trusted most and the person I always turned to for advice. We had long-term plans to live together, to rescue animals, to do the things we loved. She wanted to watch her children live out their dreams; she wanted to live out her own dreams. When she passed, my passion for poetry instantly faded. It was so quick. I couldn't write poetry. I couldn't read poetry. I couldn't even think of poetry. When I tried to so much as read a poem, I became sick to my stomach. I was numb. For the first week after my sister's passing, I stayed in bed hardly eating or drinking. Turning my body over in bed would result in a new emotional breakdown. Getting up to take a shower was hard enough. I couldn't think about living through another day. I couldn't think about living at all without my sister. It wasn't just about living day by day; it was about living minute by minute.

I have suffered from depression for most of my life, in different phases or stages. It started when I was a young child living through childhood traumas, my parent's bitter divorce, surviving a childhood where most, if not all, of the women in my immediate family were abused, some of which I witnessed first-hand. I dealt with bullying in school, body image issues, self-mutilation, and later as an adult, remained in a toxic relationship for too many years, which also led to depression. But this grief of losing my sister was more than depression, it made me realise that while the depression I experienced throughout my life up to this point was valid, it was never as intense as it was when I had to come to terms with the idea that I would never see my sister again, that I would never speak to her or get to be with her for the rest of my life. I couldn't imagine living without her. I started thinking about ending my life. This wasn't the first time. I had had suicidal thoughts many times in my three decades of life—something no one knows about, with the exception of my primary physician.

After my sister's passing, suicidal thoughts made their way into my life on a daily basis. The grief was just too overwhelming—the memories, the flashbacks of my last time seeing her face or hearing her voice. Soon after my sister passed, one of the largest fires in Northern California history forced evacuations in my home county. We had been faced with devastating wildfires for the past three years but this time, my family had to evacuate our home. There was no time to think about depression or lives ending. It was time to take action, care for our animals, care for each other and staying safe. It was a stressful time but the worst part was leaving my sister's bedroom behind, her death being so fresh and I not wanting to leave any part of her behind.

Two days into the evacuation my 14-year-old dog

Jordan who had been suffering from arthritis and dementia for nearly a year was so stressed from the evacuation that he took a turn for the worse. He stopped eating or drinking, he was moaning in pain and confusion, and couldn't sleep. I had no choice but to put him down to end his suffering. I lost my other best friend, the boy who was in my life for roughly twelve years, who lived with me through so many ups and downs. Fortunately our home was spared and we returned home a week later. Coming home to a cold, empty, ash-covered house without my sister and without my dog lead me right back into my depression, even though I was grateful to be alive and safe because others had lost much more.

All of this took place three weeks before my summer poetry reading at the farmers' market was supposed to take place. I thought about backing out. It would have been easier. But something in my gut told me my sister would have wanted me to go forward with the reading. She wanted to be there. She was excited for me. It's so hard to think of her face in a joyful manner without being brought down by the sadness which comes with remembering how she isn't in this physical world anymore, but I know the look on her face had she been able to attend this event would have been all smiles. This made me decide not to cancel the event but it didn't make it any less hard knowing she wouldn't be there. I also felt that after surviving another devastating wildfire, our county deserved to sit outside with clean air and listen to poetry after the fires had finally settled.

The day before the reading, I was receiving comments and messages via email and social media. People were excited, looking forward to such an event. I was too, but I was also heavy with sadness. I was crying for most of the day, still thinking of so much loss. I decided, to help fill some of my time since quiet only makes things worse sometimes, to bake cookies. Something about baking takes my mind off of most issues or worries. It's a sweet task to partake in when I'm feeling vulnerable but hopeful. It gives me something to do that doesn't necessarily take a lot of concentration or effort but gives soothing results. Something about cookies always makes me feel like the world is being saved and all is right, especially when others enjoy them. So I decided to bake enough for the event to treat the poets, attendees, the market manager, and for the band who played before us poets were scheduled to go on stage and who graciously shared their stage and equipment so I didn't have to rent my own.

I baked my signature vegan peanut butter cookies, my sister's favourite. I baked some vegan lemon sugar cookies and decided to throw in some pecans to make it a unique and random recipe. I packed them in pretty boxes and jars. The house smelled delicious and I had a break from tragedy for a few hours. I still cried myself to sleep that night and woke up crying the next morning. All I could think of was my sister. I didn't know how I would get through the day. But I did.

The poetry reading that day was incredible. The weather was beautiful. The smoke and ash had dissipated and the sun came out glowing, all of us humans like sunflowers looking up at its brightness. After weeks of breathing unhealthy air, we had clear air reserved for plenty of much needed deep breaths. More people came out than I expected. Children were running around playing on the grass. People were sitting in the grass and populating the picnic tables, soaking in sun and poetry. Vendors were turning around in their booths to applaud for the poets. And the best part of all was that my cookies were being passed around. From poets to friends to families, even the friends who swear off of sugar and gluten were savouring these cookies. One of my dear friends and fabulous poets also brought fresh water infused with herbs and cucumber from her garden. I made it through. With the help of friends, cookies and poems, I made it through and I was given some sort of refreshing awakening, a hint at surviving, a notion that I am doing what my sister would have wanted me to do.

Since that day I've made it a general practice to bake cookies for poetry events that I attend. Not all events, because I would be lying if I said every day still isn't as hard as the first day I learned I had lost my sister. Some days, I'm too fatigued to bake. But when I do, there is that glimmer of hope, an internal smile that I know someone is going to be made happy with this sweetness and in turn it gives my soul some warmth. I try to bake cookies for writing workshops I attend, as participants tend to especially love them. And through this I've found that living without my sister doesn't necessarily get easier, but baking for others and combining baking with my love of poetry has become a method of coping and offers a deeper sweetness and reminder that life does go on despite hardships, despite heartbreak.

Thomas Keller, proprietor of The French Laundry in Yountville said, 'A recipe has no soul. You, as the cook, must bring *soul* to the recipe.' And this is what baking often does for me, whether it's on a good day when I'm feeling great or a rough day where I have to get past a barrier of tears, it gives my final product a soul, it reignites the light in my own, it gives the day itself a replenished glow.

Recipe: Vegan Lemon Pecan Cookies

Ingredients:

1 cup vegan butter, softened

2 cups organic sugar

2 tbsp flaxseed, 6 tbsp water

1 tsp vanilla extract

1½ tbsp fresh lemon juice

1 tbsp lemon zest (or more to taste)

3 cups flour

1¼ tsp baking powder

¼ tsp baking soda

½ tsp pink Himalayan salt

1 cup pecans (or more for taste/texture)

Method:

- Preheat the oven to 350°F (180°C).
- In a large bowl, mix softened vegan butter and sugar until light and fluffy. In a separate bowl, mix flaxseed with water and once thoroughly mixed, add to butter/ sugar mixture. Add vanilla extract, fresh lemon juice, and lemon zest and mix well.
- Stir in flour, baking powder, baking soda, and salt and mix just until combined.
- Refrigerate for roughly 30 minutes or until dough is slightly firm.
- Roll into small balls and place on a baking sheet lined with parchment paper.
- Bake for 9 to11 minutes.
- Garnish with lemon zest or edible glitter for prettiness!

Mihir's Story

Jaya Vaishya

'You can't go back and change the beginning but you can
start where you are and change the ending.'
—C.S. Lewis

I got married at the age of twenty-five, full of hope and excitement to start a family. It was a good life, a happy life and in just a year there was the wonderful news of my pregnancy. However, the story diverged from the norm right from the moment Mihir was born. From his delivery, to his development, to the way he moved, heard and communicated, Mihir was different. Diagnosed with athetoid cerebral palsy, neural hearing sensory loss coupled with intellectual disability, he had a multitude of factors that set him apart.

It was very hard at first. I had never dealt with something like this before but Mihir is one of those extraordinary people who doesn't let his disabilities define him. He shows great resilience and strength, which inspires everyone. Over the years we have developed our own method of communication, which involves a lot of hand gestures. We have our own special ways of understanding one another.

When Mihir was five years old, he started attending Jai Vakeel School in Mumbai. In school, he excelled at craft even though he didn't have full control of his movements. He didn't let his hearing issues come in the way of pursuing dance, something he absolutely loves. Even when it came to socialising and making friends, Mihir managed to make heads turn in spite of difficulty in communicating. Mihir always followed his heart and his abilities have adapted to his interests.

Due to his artistic skills, Mihir moved from the school section to the Vocational Training Section at the age of eighteen. He was first put in the incense-making class where he was taught how to make aromatic incense sticks. After a few years, he was reassessed and shifted to the paper craft section of the Skill Development Centre, which he still currently goes to, and enjoys thoroughly. At Jai Vakeel, he has friends and the chance to interact with new people and learn different things. To have a schedule and have friends has made a major difference in his life.

Five years ago, we ran into a financial crunch. The shop we ran for generations was taken away from us. After a lot of advice and having received compliments for my cooking skills for years, I ventured into a tiffin service to earn money.

At home, Mihir is fairly independent and does most of the household work. He even goes around the neighbourhood by himself. But for years I had no idea that he had an innate talent, a passion that I thought would be beyond his reach. Mihir absolutely loves to cook. This secret talent only came to light when, on an absolute whim, I applied to the Veruschka Foundation, a space that trains children with special needs to become independent chefs. Before that, I had never let Mihir come near the stove or even hold a knife. I was too afraid that he may get confused or injure himself.

When Mihir goes into the kitchen he wants to do everything himself. He has always been hard-working and takes pride in everything he does, and this is reflected in his cooking too. It is funny how I had never allowed him to hold a knife before, but his knife skills are something that I now envy.

Mihir has a few disruptive behaviours and can sometimes be very stubborn. However, when he is in the kitchen and cooking, he never has any issues. He is calm, and sometimes even when angry, cools down by himself. I remember times when he was upset with me for some reason or sulking and I would go into the kitchen to finish off my work, Mihir would come up to me quietly and nudge me. After making a subtle gesture, he would slowly take what was in my hand and start completing it himself.

He loves to watch me cook and has the ability to pick up cooking skills. His knowledge of cooking really expanded though, due to the Veruschka Foundation where he learnt to make new dishes like aloo chat, dosa, Chinese fried rice and vegetable Manchurian. His current favourite dish is bhindi masala and roti, something he recently learnt.

The pride I feel when he completes a dish all by himself or the joy I see on his face when he presents something he has made is quite something—very hard to put into words. To see Mihir's smile is like sunshine on a rainy day! It lights up his face and brings joy to the room.

There is a sort of calmness that I see on his face whenever he is in the kitchen. I'd like to think his passion for cooking comes from me.

Mihir has always been positive and happy despite the hardships he faces and, as a mother, that gives me the greatest strength, that stops the internal chatter of 'why me'. When he brings his maximum effort to the table, it inspires me to do more, be better.

Recipe: Mihir's Bhindi Masala

Ingredients:

450 gm bhindi (okra), trimmed
2 tbsp oil
1 large tomato, finely chopped
1 large onion, chopped
3-4 garlic cloves, finely chopped
½ tsp cumin seed
¼ tsp garam masala powder (optional)
½ tsp red chili powder
¼ tsp turmeric powder
1 tsp coriander powder
Salt
1 tbsp coriander leaves, finely chopped

Method:

- Wash bhindi in water and dry it using cloth or paper napkin. If possible, complete this process 2 to 3 hours prior to cooking.
- Remove its head and tail and chop it into small round slices of about 1 cm.
- Heat oil in a non-stick pan or heavy-based kadhai (rounded vessel).
- Add cumin seeds Jand when they begin to crackle, add chopped garlic and chopped onions. Sauté for 30 seconds. Add chopped bhindi and mix well.
- Cook on medium-low flame until bhindi turns dark green and shrinks. It will take approximately 6 to 8 minutes. Stir occasionally.

- Add chopped tomatoes, turmeric powder and salt; cook until tomatoes turn tender, approximately 2 minutes.
- Add red chilli powder, garam masala powder and coriander powder; mix well.
- Cook for a minute over low flame and turn off the flame. Transfer prepared bhindi bhaji to a serving bowl.
- Garnish with coriander leaves.

Recipe for Chapati:

Ingredients:

1 cup whole wheat flour + 2 tbsp flour for rolling chapatis
50 ml water or more if needed
½ to ¾ tsp salt
1 tsp oil
½ cup ghee

Method:

- Sieve the whole wheat flour into a bowl. Add salt and 1 tsp oil and start mixing the dough. Continue to knead the dough and keep on adding water as required.
- Knead the dough till it becomes pliable and soft; the final dough consistency should not be soft or hard. Divide the dough into equal pieces, enough dough to make it a little larger than a golf ball, and roll each piece in the palms of your hands to form balls.
- Flatten the balls and sprinkle some wheat flour on the dough; make round chapatis with a rolling pin. Once the tawa gets hot, put the chapati and cook on both sides till you get brown spots.
- Take the chapati off the fire, place on a plate and apply some ghee with a spoon.

Cooking with Some Help through Bipolar Disorder

Devika Menon

I had never been a kitchen person while growing up. The kitchen was never solace, and I didn't pay much attention to what was on my plate. I come from a relatively privileged background, and have always had someone else cook for me. My mother has been working since as long as I can remember, and she really wasn't the type of mother who cooked for the whole family. My father too never really took any interest in the matter. Cooking was almost always delegated to the household help of the time. My grandmother, however, loved to cook, but I came to love her cooking much later in life.

Things changed when I moved out of home for a year in 2009, to work at a rural non-profit in a small mountain village. I was forced to start with the basics—how to put on the lid of the pressure cooker, basic masalas (red chilli powder, turmeric, coriander powder), how to boil rice, and how to make simple vegetables and lentils. Cooking here was more about survival, and also a fun community activity to participate in with other staff members and volunteers. My lovely flatmate and friends were helpful on this journey, and it is possible that the seeds of my future cooking journey were sown here.

I left the NGO in 2010 to pursue a Master's degree programme. Unfortunately, things didn't work out, as I went through my second bipolar disorder episode. I was first diagnosed with bipolar disorder as a 17-year-old, and back then, I didn't really understand what was going on. I came out of that episode, not knowing that I would be in the same place five years later. This time however, I knew what was going on, but life just seemed to carry on with no meaning. I never felt like getting out of bed, and I tried to force myself to sleep. Terrible, terrible thoughts would play on my mind, including repeatedly telling myself that I was a failure for dropping out of the Master's programme. I even considered suicide at one point. Somehow, I got the courage to carry on.

One day, out of the blue, I started a cooking blog. I set out on a blogging challenge, and set myself a target of cooking daily for ninety days. This really gave me courage, and it was through this blogging journey that I was able to nurse myself back to my old, functional happy self. The blog's title, *Cooking With Some Help*, was a testament to the other people in my life who helped me cook or encouraged me—our housemaid Sujita, her toddler daughter, my dogs Zulu and Zorro, my parents, and all my friends and relatives who actually read the blog every day. Come hell or high water, I used to blog. Feeling tired, feeling sleepy, meeting a friend, travelling to other cities, none of these was a deterrent. The blog showed me and others my spirit of resilience.

As I cooked and cooked some more, the blues slowly and steadily went away. I gained confidence, and learnt about new and interesting ingredients. These included haloumi cheese, which I felt was very similar to the paneer you can get at any dairy, or the seasonality of the vegetables we are so fortunate to have access to in India. I learnt how to make avial, a mixed vegetable dish from Kerala, from my grandmother, how to make a delicious sausage salad from another friend, and some really soothing mutton curry, whose recipe given by a dear friend included 'whacking' the mutton! One day, running out of ideas, I made cinnamon butter toast, which was beautiful in how simple it was!

I continued cooking. I made a ring-mould cake, and used a glass to make the ring, a stellar idea from my grandmother! I even attempted a red velvet cake, which was not as ubiquitous as it is today. Both these recipes were from a popular chef who actually wrote in to me telling me how kind I was. This truly made my day. I even made fifty-five cupcakes for my niece's birthday in the park! From someone who couldn't get out of bed, to a proactive person making so many cupcakes on a single day—I had certainly come a long way because of my blogging!

The act of entering the kitchen space daily, with so much interest, was such a drastic change from my childhood and adolescent years. Those ninety days of cooking daily changed who I was as a person, and gave my life the meaning and direction it needed at that time. Along with the blues going away, I awakened my inner cooking queen. Some years later, it was where my career would take me as well.

I went on to do my Master's from a UK-based development institute, and even there, I loved talking about food and feeding others! Again in 2013, the bipolar bug bit me badly. The same blues were back, and this time, I was under a deadline to write a dissertation. However I chose wisely and perhaps that was the start of my healing. I based my dissertation on a local masala centre, where I interviewed the women making masalas. This process of talking to them daily, and inhaling all the spices, was a part of the healing process.

After pursuing my Master's, I started work at a non-profit, foraying back into the development sector. However, something was amiss. I didn't enjoy going to work at all, and it became a task to force myself out of bed each morning.

When I could take it no more, I quit my job, and started working at a café inside a lovely arts studio! Along with my co-workers, I came up with a tiny, compact menu full of all things good. From cooking out of my home kitchen to actually managing a canteen, I had come a long way.

I eventually quit working at the canteen, and started my own baking business in 2019, called Phool Kumari Bakes. Now, when I bake and frost and ice and pack orders, I am truly in my element. I can safely say that cooking has and always will be my *raison d'être*.

RECIPE: MAMBRAKOOTAN (FLAVOURSOME MANGO CURRY)

This is a traditional dish from Kerala. My grandmother made it every year on the important festivals of Onam and Vishu (along with many other delicacies).

Serves 3

Ingredients:

3 ripe mangoes
1 tsp turmeric
Salt to taste
1 tsp cumin seeds
½ tsp pepper

Half a coconut
1 green chilli
300 gm yoghurt

For the tempering:

1 tbsp coconut oil
1 tsp black mustard seeds
1 whole red chilli
2-3 fenugreek (methi) seeds
2-3 curry leaves

Method:

- Boil the pulp of the mangoes with turmeric and salt. Grate the coconut. Roast the cumin seeds.
- Grind roasted cumin seeds, pepper, grated coconut and green chilli together.
- Add it to the cooked mango, and cook for 2 to 3 minutes.
- Add yoghurt (lightly beaten) and stir.
- Heat the oil for tempering (tadka). Add the mustard seeds and let them splutter. Immediately add the red chilli, fenugreek seeds and curry leaves. Add this to the cooked mango curry.
- Serve with plain boiled rice.

POETRY AND NARRATIVES

Ode to Khichdi

Kashiana Singh

I remember
reborn into myself
bursting and blooming
a child splendorous in my arms
an ache fevering itself into my nights

I remember
bursting into tears
tears that never stopped
my shadows emptying my selves
through a 40-day hiatus of unreeled days

I remember
the need to renew
my loneliness flowing naked
into my pores as they blossomed
with bruises of birth, hormones of relief

I remember
in need for the sweet nectar
to enliven my sagging breasts
parched of hunger and sleep
being cradled in a contagious wakefulness

I remember, a stew
its stickiness bountiful
a celebration of stamina
tempering my tears
I remember, a lush
yellow broth, luminous
with diced garlic, simmering
into a thicket, cooked nostalgia

I remember, wholesome
round lentils splitting
drizzling gold, an ever
unnoticed turmeric

I remember a jubilance of
shredded ginger placated by ghee
split panch daals courting rice grains
maverick peppercorns and jeera
garnished with a dash of coriander

I remember, ma
As composed as yogurt and mint
bringing a matki
laden with warmth
simmering unperturbed
with ghee and affirmation

her pot ever bubbling
with a nudging silence
of khichdi
khichdi of nudging certainty
each spoon purging me of bile

Recipe: Khichdi

Ingredients:

1 to 2 tbsp ghee
½ to ¾ tsp cumin seeds (jeera)
1 tsp ginger grated, pressed, or finely chopped
1 green chilli, slit
½ tsp red chili powder
⅛ tsp turmeric
Salt as needed
½ cup rice (any rice)
½ cup moong daal
3 to 4 cups water (use more for a more liquid
    consistency)
Chopped hara dhania (cilantro), about 1 tsp
½ tbsp ghee for topping

Method:

- Add rice and daal to a pot. Wash them twice and drain the water completely.
- Heat the ghee in a pressure cooker or pot on medium heat. Add cumin seeds and sauté it on a low flame. Then fry ginger until fragrant and sprinkle cilantro.
- If desired, add carrots, beans, salt and turmeric. Sauté for 3 to 4 minutes.
- Add drained daal and rice. Pour 3 cups water for mush like consistency
- Cook until soft adding more water if needed. If using a pressure cooker, three whistles on a slow heat should be enough. If using a pot, cover and cook on simmer for 20 to 30 minutes, until the daal is tender.
- Pour 1 tsp ghee on the hot khichdi.
- Serve with papad and raw mango pickle.

Food Porn

Juhi Kalra

Breakfast

Eggs, beaten till they beg for mercy. Onions, ginger and serrano sautéed in the febrile butter til- l they are languid with pleasure. Pan sputtering as the golden liquid moves about its surface, gelling and setting in ecstasy. Spinach and cheese placed in the centrefold, gently covered over with tender loving care, the whole of it folded, lifted ever so gently, clinging to the spatula, and sliding effortlessly onto the yearning Pfaltzgraff, cilantro sitting atop the creation like a tiara. An Omelette fit for a Queen.

Cardamom ginger tea too hot to sip. Heaven…aaaah.

Lunch

The bread was sturdy, aware of its youth but not arrogant about it. Two rough-hewn slices landed confidently in the sizzling pan, daring it to tan them. Delicate white slices of mozzarella and provolone cheese lay on top of the bread, melting in quiet shyness. Thin slices of ruby tomato, red onion, and green peppers joined the bacchanal, wilting in the bliss of chilli and cilantro raining down on them. Finally, a spatula sliding under them, the two sides coming together with a satisfied thud. Panini stood around the pan like an audience at the conclusion of Madame Butterfly, applauding but green with envy, as the hot creation slid off the spatula smoothly and into the arms of the waiting Waterford, resting in the knowledge of its perfection. A knife sliced through its rectangular heart diagonally, and the hand turned the two halves around to make a perfect heart. A Kent mango, a sorry substitute for its Indian cousin, the langda, sat forlorn at the counter. The hand picked it up lovingly, gently bathing it in a cool spray at the sink.

A knife ran around the rim of the head, where the stem had connected this mango to the tree, and removed the remains of its umbilicus. Round and round went the knife, disrobing the mango, leisurely in one long string of skin that fell like a stripper's cover up when the bottom tip of the paisley was reached. The hand scoured the mango all around its circumference, letting the golden goodness slide around in its own juices. Julienned strips were cut, and fanned out by the side of the warm sandwich heart, ready to be devoured. And they were, leaving a trail of golden liquid dripping from the lips.

Dinner

The door of the fridge flung open, small containers of leftovers retrieved.

Drying vegetable kababs went on the greasy pan, not yet ready in its heat to receive them. A soupy concoction that once had been a passable curry was dumped unsung into a microwave safe bowl and tossed into the square of nuking energy for two minutes. By the time a frozen tortilla was thrown into the toaster oven, the kababs were smoking. When the timer sang on the microwave, the liquid in the curry had spilled or burned off, leaving pieces of malai kofta sticking to the sides of the bowl.

The tortilla came out of the toaster crisper than a freshly minted dollar bill, having sat in its heated home while clean Melamine was hunted for in the once pristine kitchen.

There was no finesse in the presentation, but sometimes a quickie bite is all one needs after a long hard day before falling asleep. And even bad food can be good when we're hungry.

How I Healed Myself through Food

In three hours one Sunday morning in the summer of 2008, I wrote a series of fifteen poems. They are some of my favourite work.

In the autumn of 2007, I had begun to have tactile memories of being molested at a preverbal age. I knew this because the child sharing these memories with me had no words to articulate what she was experiencing. Instead she stood by the side of my bed and allowed me to feel on my body what she was feeling on hers. I believe this scared the pants off my then husband with whom I had spent the last thirty-five years.

Within six months, he had gone off to explore new career opportunities elsewhere in the state where we lived, leaving me mentally and physically broken, and alone not for the first time in our long marriage.

I joined the UCLA (University of California, Los Angeles) Extension Writing Program that spring and found myself in a creative writing class with an instructor who was like no teacher I had ever had! Her hair was blacker than black, she had tattoos everywhere, she looked at least thirty years younger than me, and she had a strong New York accent. Turned out she was as sweet and tart as a cherry rugelach, and exactly what I needed. My memories came pouring out on paper in her Wednesday night classes, some recounted from having been always in my conscious memory, some just hitting me out of the blue from the unknown depths of my subconscious. Lots of poetry came out in that class.

My then partner, now ex, came home every few months but I was completely unable to be the wife to whom he had grown accustomed. I was no good in the bed anymore where he felt no longer welcome. I was no good in the kitchen which he had never deigned to learn to navigate. What I was really good for, except lying around half-undressed in an unkempt house all day, was reading and writing and crying. Then one fateful weekend after months of not cooking, I decided to make us breakfast. Limping on my torn knee, leaning on crutches, I travelled from living room to kitchen. I remember writing a poem, tossing the notebook into his lap, hobbling to the kitchen, starting a segment of the meal, returning to write another poem, tossing the notebook into his lap again, returning to the kitchen again. This went on for three hours. No matter how complicated a meal, no matter how many items on the menu, it has never taken me three hours to make breakfast before or since that day!

I think this may have been the day he decided I was a goner, he was never getting 'wifey' back, he better skedaddle and get the hell out of town for good! And so he eventually stopped coming home, leaving me with a broken body and fragmented mind to figure my life out by myself at the ripe old age of almost fifty-five.

On a trip to India in 2009 I went through a phase of having to move between friends' homes every few days. Some evenings, hours were spent reminiscing about time spent together in college, years ago, parts of which I had forgotten and needed reminding of, some easily remembered with nostalgic pleasure. Catching up on years spent apart yet so similar, of lives lived without choice or purpose, other than to struggle through each day. Of husbands and their no-good-ness, having had enough of living under duress, with few options and fewer pleasures. Of husbands no longer in the picture, some regretfully, some gratefully, some with ambivalence. We spoke of children who had become saviours and adult friends, often cheering us on to those liberties in life they themselves had achieved. Some clung to their children as their own mothers and mothers-in-law had, not seeing the similarities in their inability to let go. Some watched their adult children from afar with an aching pride, wishing them back in their homes and daily lives. And the rare mother who lived with only the memory of her child, never having seen her grow to adulthood.

In Delhi, I found meals prepared by kitchen help to varying degrees of competence. Not often having worked alone in their own kitchens, my friends had nothing to compare with how marvellous food could taste when prepared with knowledge and caring. I found myself being more accepting of the middle-aged medical wives in Los Angeles who passed off catered meals as their own home-cooked, just as I saw meals supplemented in Delhi with store-bought sides and additions. I laugh at my own judgmental self who took such pride in doing everything well from scratch, in tiny towns across the Midwest and East Coast of America, when I had no choice but to learn to do it that way.

We laugh together, and I break into crying as I confide why I am in Delhi, and why this trip is different than any other before. In some homes I feel safe, protected, nurtured.

Led through the intricacies of how what works: the secrets of geysers and hot water for showers, electric outlets, light switches and what they turn on, which drapes and doors it is safer to keep closed. How the internet is accessible in their homes: my one absolute need, next only to bottled or boiled water. Bathrooms provided with all necessities, like a good hotel. Towels laid out on the bed with extra blankets. The soiled pillow I have taken to carrying everywhere with me laid with acceptance next to their own pristine linens. In other homes, I can see that I overwhelm them with my pain and they, being overwhelmed with it, treat me with cautious disregard. I knock around not knowing how anything works, where anything is kept, how to make my own cup of morning tea, or call my own cab from someone only they are in the know with. I have friends who have sat on their haunches, covering my bug-bitten legs and dirty feet with Odomos and Off, putting bug-away products into electric sockets at night, spraying repellent around my bed an hour before bedtime so that it has time to penetrate the little buggers where they hide. And others who marvelled at my pock-marked mosquito-bitten face in the morning, not once doing anything to prevent its repetition on subsequent nights in their own guest rooms. And I have not known how to ask. I hobbled into their homes with my injured knee, and some have taken to walking me around their property holding my elbow and my hand; putting heating pads and hot water bottles into my bed, wrapping crepe bandages around my swollen leg against my protests. Others, whose own life consumes them, lovingly include me in their social engagements, then leave me to my own devices, where I climb multiple stairwells to be part of festive merrymaking, and am met with surprise from my hosts that anything was impeding my mobility at all.

Every night as I lay my head down on my now dirty pillow, my companion, the mosquito, comes to me. He buzzes around my head, looking for exposed fleshy parts of my juicy body. I have learned to hide everything under sheets and blankets, tucking them all around me as a parent may have done with an adored child. Yet as I drift off to slumber, a finger protruding from my cocoon is duly bitten. Or the lip or the nose or the cheek or the forehead on the side left open for breathing. Sometimes I find him in the morning, drunk with my blood, lying next to my head on the pillow. Some mornings I find him smashed, surrounded by my blood, perhaps slapped by my sleeping scratching hand.

But most mornings, he is nowhere to be found, hibernating in my hair or my clothes or my soul, just waiting for night to fall again, so that he can play his game with me. And I play the game gladly, knowing not he or anything else in this crowded city will force me away until I have excised all my ghosts, the ghosts of my perpetrators. And his buzzing is my wake-up call.

After that trip to Delhi, and many years of concerted intentional living to acknowledge and overcome my childhood trauma of sexual abuse and violence, which I recognised made the abuse in my single adult relationship inevitable, I reclaimed my ability to cook. I began by cooking for myself at first, finding the foods that all my younger dissociated personae wished to eat. With each step in my own healing, my ability to nurture others with food as I had learned to do for myself, returned. Eventually, cooking became my language in communicating and sharing my love with those who came into my life. Being surrounded by other survivors, especially LGBTQ people and people of colour in a predominantly white community has become my norm. Eventually, quite organically, teaching cooking to others evolved. I launched a not-for-profit business teaching trauma-informed cooking to survivors of patriarchy within the South Asian diaspora in California. I charge no money for the classes, and take no more than two students at a time, and only if they know each other. Although I do not practice therapy with them, knowing their triggers and exploring how they wish to nurture their own bodies has a lasting impact on my students' propensity for learning. Many young women react to forced patriarchal chains by not learning to do anything considered 'women's work' by their families and communities. Many young men are not offered the opportunity to learn self- sustenance. Eventually, they realise that eating out takes a big chunk of their income, way beyond their resources. This is how they find their way to me, because learning to cook in classes offered at community colleges and culinary schools do not address the reasons why they don't cook to begin with.

When I see others' trauma without flinching, I find acceptance and release of my own trauma. When I support others in their healing, my own healing accelerates. When a student makes a meal to feed themselves for the first time, my spirit is fed with their gratitude and my own gratitude increases beyond measure. There is nothing altruistic about altruism. I do what I do because it increases my joy a thousand-fold. I wouldn't have it any other way.

Recipe: Juhi's Desi Tofu Loaf

Being vegetarian, for our American Thanksgiving meal in November we had everything but the turkey for fifteen years.

With vegetarianism then sweeping the nation a faux turkey product called Tofurky became available in stores. The first time we tried it was also our last! The next holiday I put together the beginning of this recipe which, over the years, has evolved into a marvellous meal on its own. This recipe has gained so much popularity that I often make two loaf pans so we are sure to have leftovers for the day after.

This dish can be prepared the night before, and baked an hour before serving. Tastes great warm, room temperature or cold and is great the next day in a sandwich just like leftover turkey! We call it Desi Tofu Loaf.

Prepare the tofu earlier to save time when assembling. If you want a more 'turkey' taste, substitute two heaped teaspoons of good quality poultry or Italian seasoning for the Indian masala.

Ingredients:

800 gm extra-firm tofu
¾ cup shredded carrots
1-1½ cups of red or white onion, finely diced
1 serrano or jalapeño chilli (or equivalent), finely chopped
1 inch fresh ginger, peeled and grated
Handful cilantro, chopped
1 heaped tsp cumin, ground
1 heaped tsp salt, or to taste
1 heaped tsp coriander, ground
½ tsp turmeric (haldi)
A big pinch of asafoetida (hing)

½ cup fresh or dried ground breadcrumbs
1 whole egg, lightly beaten
I tbsp orange juice

Method:

- Remove tofu from packaging, drain in colander. Wrap tofu in kitchen towel, cloth (not paper). Place a weighted pot on top of tofu in a colander for 1 to 2 hours to further drain liquid out of tofu.
- Make sure tofu is completely dry before adding other ingredients.
- Add onions, carrots, chilli (or 1 tsp dry cayenne for even heat as a personal preference), ginger, cilantro, egg and all seasonings. Mix thoroughly.
- Lightly grease 8-inch loaf pan and fill with tofu mixture. Pat down tightly.
- Bake in a 350°F (180°C) oven for 45-55 mins, until the top begins to brown and no liquid is bubbling on the sides.
- Allow to sit for 30-45 minutes to set.
- The loaf can be inverted onto a lovely serving plate for garnishing, or sliced right out of the loaf pan.
- Make sure to allow the loaf to cool completely if inverting, so it does not fall apart!

The Picnic

Sue Flowers

'Stop eating your emotions mum' he said…
He was right of course.
I couldn't stop piling in the comfort creams
And woeful waffles.
Next came the exhausted éclairs and melancholy meringues.
After that I spread a whole tub of sadness
On a loaf of kindness.
It completely ruined the taste.

I knew it was bad for me,
But I couldn't stop,
So I made a great pile of sandwiches
Out of some left over resentment
And decided to go out.

I was just about to leave when
I found a packet of freshly baked worries,
They were just perfect…
Out of their centres oozed Anxiety, Fear, Love and Hatred,
Excitement and Sorrow
All contained within their own little shortbread cases.

After eating these I decided to pack a picnic.
My basket was overflowing with so much to take;
Loneliness, Anxiety, Happiness, Sadness
Kindness and Love.
I'd have a big shop to do next week
To replace all of those,
But I was determined to use everything up.

Then off I went to the river, all on my own,
With a lovely large basket full of emotions.
I was quite tired when I finally got there.
As I arrived I felt the air so clear,
The light dazzling my appetite
And I watched the swifts in the sky
Unthreading their invisible celestial tapestry.

That was the moment I realised
I wasn't hungry at all.
So I picked up the basket,
Breathed in the beauty
And emptied all of its contents into the river.

The best day of my life, that was.
I'd kept the love and kindness in my pocket
For the walk home.

Making Soup

When I make a soup it is created and shared with love.

Sometimes just the choosing of the soup that I hope to make for someone else can give me a deep warm feeling in the centre of my stomach. I imagine others tasting it and feeling nourished by what I make. It makes me feel good to think I've undertaken a small act of kindness, and by the making of soup, I feel more connected to others.

Making soup can be a great way to heal in emotionally turbulent times and a pragmatic solution to putting food on the table. The recipes aren't complex and there's a therapeutic element to the repetitive chopping, boiling and stirring required. It is also perfectly okay if I get distracted and go to do something else, because it never seems to spoil, the longer it boils the tastier my soup seems to become.

As I cook, I develop a kind of symbiosis with the soup; my emotions move into the soup and the soup-making becomes a part of me. For me, this kind of cooking feels like magic, a natural alchemy for the soul. For I do believe that taking a simple handful of raw vegetables and making them into a rich and tasty broth can achieve a transformation of the mind.

In our home, where the old maroon Rayburn cooker is always on the go (like me) I think there is nothing better than to pile a load of fresh ingredients into a pan and let the mixture slowly simmer itself into a nourishing soup whilst I get on with my working day.

I start by plunging my hands into ice-cold water, washing and peeling the vegetables. Immediately I realise that I can't think about all of the other things going on in my life and swirling around in my brain, when my fingers are freezing. The coldness of the water reminds me of the freshness of picking vegetables from a winter garden and my mind naturally wanders to outdoor memories. It is when the weather turns colder that I find my mind turning towards soup making to remember the pleasure of bringing nature indoors and creating something new out of something so simple.

For me, making soup is like creating a culinary tapestry for the soul; far more important than the recipes or ingredients is the time spent giving and caring and creating with commitment.

I particularly noticed a need to make soup when I was in an emotional crisis after my father passed away. I felt so helpless, I wanted to do something, anything, I wanted to help those around me and I also needed to find a way to manage my mind, which I felt was slowly and surely going into a meltdown. I knew I couldn't do anything about his passing, he had gone, but I could try to use my emotions to help the family around me, and so I made soup.

Providing nourishment for those who were grieving seemed to help me. I hoped my soup would remind others that there was still life and that it was precious. And whilst grief had made our lives difficult, we still needed to look after ourselves and eat, even if we didn't feel hungry. I hoped that in some small way, by nourishing our bodies, my culinary art might help to nourish our emotions at the same time. I only make warm soups, because I think they are soups for the soul; cold soups such as gazpacho don't really speak to me, as I think I need to pass on the warmth of caring with my soup. I now realise that in times of joy and deep sorrow I turn to making soup—it seems to ease my soul.

During difficult and complex times making soup always gives me something to focus on. 'Wash the celery and peel the potatoes, get that done first,' I tell myself. 'Melt the butter and chop the onion, boil the kettle and see if we have any stock cubes.'

The order of the recipe gives my mind a much-needed temporary routine, providing time to focus and a simple space to be whilst I am immersed in the doing of it.

One of the first soups I ever made was pumpkin and

orange soup, vats of which were made for our wedding-day feast. I've always loved the bright autumnal light, kicking leaves about in the woodland and the celebratory harvest produce brought into church for harvest festivals, and so along with our autumnal commitment to each other, we made our very own harvest feast.

Before the feast, our time was well-spent scooping out pumpkin flesh from their outer casings, ensuring there was enough produce to make pumpkin pies and pans full of bright orange pumpkin soup. In the hall where we danced and shared our joy, the oranges, yellows, greens and blood red of flowers and foliage danced out of their jam jars and vases, whilst the pumpkin lanterns illuminated the simple meal that we all enjoyed together. Little did I know that this emotional way of cooking—expressing my love through the making of soup—would be the start of something yet to come.

During our early married life, money was scarce, so visits to the Lune valley to gather damsons and apples from my parents' orchard led me to seek out interesting ways of using freely available produce from their garden; and so parsnip and apple soup was born and quickly became one of our favourites.

As my family grew, I was happy to cook large pans full of soup to be served and distributed to relatives. Whether ill, old or unhappy I shared my soothing soups and I quickly learnt that soup freezes fantastically and is a great meal to take out in small portions when someone is unwell or on rainy days when you don't want to go out.

Being regularly lost in thought whilst making soup is not problematic. I can forget all about the pan left slowly simmering on the hob, but it never lets me down and burns.

Despite such occasional memory lapses, when I am greeted by flutters of panic, I find that they are always unfounded, and that my soup will be still waiting for me whenever I would like to give it my full attention. So, when I return to the kitchen to hastily pull the pan from the hob, I return to my focus, blending, adjusting flavours and consistency, and trying to make things just right. I can vouch for this reliability of soup, for it will undoubtedly always be waiting for me to 'finish it off'; whether that requires thinning, thickening, seasonings, herbs or dollops of crème fraiche.

Making soup provides nourishment for the mind, body and soul; and for me it has always provided a deep sense of meaning and a wider sense of emotional purpose. At times of helplessness and crisis I turn to make soup. When a loved one has died, there is no turning back the clock, nothing to be done, and yet at the same time there is always so much to be done. So, within the tidal wave of grief and trauma I seek out solace in the kitchen.

Soup is quite literally a mind-altering substance, the making, giving and sharing of which can fill you with joy. So, if you haven't tried making soup yet, you might just want to give it a go…A soup and a new you are born. Enjoy!

RECIPES

For making soup you will need a heat source, a pan, a blender, and a wooden spoon.

CELERY AND POTATO SOUP

Ingredients:

50 gm butter

1 medium onion, finely chopped

1 large leafy head of celery, finely chopped
450 gm potatoes, peeled and sliced
710 ml of light chicken or vegetable stock (stock cubes
    are fine to use, but I usually use twice as many for
    soup)
Salt and pepper to taste

Method:

- Melt the butter in a large saucepan then add the onion, celery and potatoes. Cover and cook gently for around 10 minutes ensuring the vegetables don't brown.
- Add the stock and season well. Cover the pan and bring to the boil, simmer gently for about 30 minutes or until all the vegetables are tender.
- Allow it to cool a little; you may add some cold water now, as the mixture will need thinning. Process half of the soup in a blender until it is smooth. The other half should be barely processed so that it remains coarse.
- Return the soup to the pan and adjust for seasoning. Check the consistency—if too thick you may like to add more water, milk, or a little cream.
- Reheat gently and serve piping hot, ideally with fresh wholemeal bread.

Parsnip and Apple Soup

Ingredients:

25 gm butter
1 medium onion, finely chopped
2 medium-sized parsnips
1 medium-sized cooking apple
600 ml of vegetable stock

2 tbsp (30 ml) chopped fresh parsley
½ tsp (2.5 ml) dried mixed dried herbs
355 ml semi-skimmed milk
Salt and pepper to taste

Method:

- Chop the apple and vegetables. Melt the butter in a large pan and sauté them all together, stirring frequently until the onion is transparent. Add the stock and herbs and bring to the boil. Cover, reduce the heat and allow to simmer for 30 minutes. Add the milk and allow to cool a little before using a soup blender and blending until smooth. Reheat to serving temperature and adjust seasoning to taste.

Give Back Your Heart/To Itself

Sumayyah Malik

(After Derek Walcott's 'Love After Love')

hey love, today is the perfect day to
stroll and let your sketchy bones crackle
and sunbathe into the warm cuddle
of self-acceptance that was hidden in
the coffin of too-much that the darkness
of it suffocated you and your
yawn and stretch.

i will dress you up in the silk of
sunlit rays from the purification to
the creek of your vessels. i will buy you
a floral tiara to make your wretched atrium
look pretty. i will lemonade your bitter skeleton
to the sour of your blood. just to make your veins
blush, we will make this work.

we will greet today, over the toast of
imperfect coffee with added sugar
ointments and less of fair-milkiness
in it. we will light up the stray candle
that looks like a cabbage but smells like a

porridge of love. we will smudge each
other right in this room in the
unison of acceptance.
because I give my heart to itself.

RECIPE: DALGONA COFFEE

Ingredients:

> 2 tbsp sugar
> 2 tbsp Nescafe coffee
> 2 tbsp cold water
> 1 cup milk

Method:

- In your favourite mug given by your best friend/lover/
  parent/co-worker, combine sugar, self-love, coffee,
  strength and water. Vigorously beat it until the mixture
  turns a smooth mixture of rusty sunshine, then continue
  whisking until it thickens to a dusty cotton cloud.
- Fill a glass with milk, then dollop and swirl the whipped
  coffee mixture on top, mix it before drinking. Sip it and:

Give back your heart/to itself

FICTION

Aranygaluska

Tamás Dávid-Barrett

*(All individual characters and personal events
depicted in this story are fictional.)*

I

It was after many months of friendship, maybe a year, that I invited Ömer to come to our place for a dinner party.

He was the son of conservative Ottoman elite, and he was fat, gay, and dedicated to the past. His moustache was the first thing I noticed about him, like most other people, I guess. I couldn't help but focus on his lip's furry outpourings escaping the face and advertising well ahead, the arrival of the actual Ömer.

The fact that he was an Oxford professor of history was also impossible to miss. This way or that, he wove this CV element into every fifth sentence, even when discussing the misdeeds of colonialism while walking down the Thames path, our regular post-lunch half hour. We often ended up sitting in the Rose and Crown despite the English ale nationalism they serve there by the earful. He whispered that he liked to have sex with other men. Maybe so because of the fear he experienced in Turkey as a teenager, or maybe because his homosexual desires were entirely aspirational.

I was entertained by this man with his wobbly steps and constant awareness of the princely privilege he grew up with. And the fact that he chose a life of an intellectual in a city in which nobody gave a first fuck about the noble titles you might have had in 'a faraway country about which we know little'. This was how the British PM, Chamberlain, described Czechoslovakia as he threw the country into the arms of Hitler. The birthplace of Ömer being even further away and even less known.

He was the first to issue a social invite. It was a Eurovision song contest evening, an event we watched in his small North Oxford apartment, an odd group of nerds. I thought it was rather inclusive of him that, wanting to counterbalance the cringe that takes over my body in the presence of such music, he also put on the Goldberg Variations via a loudspeaker in the background. This created a combined effect of designer junk pop and the mathematical pleasures of this particularly genius Bach piece on loop. I felt as if I were a reptile urgently needing to shed its skin from burning heat on one side and ice-cold wind on the other.

In return, I invited him back. It was not, however, one of those naturally flowing dinner parties. Apart from Ömer and my wife Alice, we also had an Irish war correspondent, Kieran. He had spent so much time overtly covering, and covertly assassinating the elites of various Middle Eastern countries for the British government, that the contradictions this chubby red-haired man carried baffled even the most nomadly of us. I mean how can you live like that, we all asked, to which this son of Dublin volunteered the prescription of frequent whiskey delivery from the homeland.

To top it all, we had a tank enthusiast, too. He was an exceedingly pale-skinned Englishman. Tall and frail in a way that defied his actual mid-thirties age by at least forty years. He was a would-be first date for Ömer, we gathered, although the relationship was unlikely to be consummated due to their very visible lack of interest in each other's physical manifestation. His name was Colin, perhaps, but I might have just made that up. I sometimes see him on the streets of Oxford. He shyly puts his head down, and looks away, always sideways, as if he was still embarrassed by what he witnessed at that dinner some twelve years ago. Which is a pity, for I still want to ask him what's so interesting about tanks.

I had cooked some meat with veggies for the omnivores, and veggies with veggies for the plant-eaters, and one dessert dish to be shared from the middle of the table.

II

This sweet dish was special food, for special people on special occasions. My grandmother, Nana, used to make it for me, or rather for our small family. She, a widow, along with my aunt, a life-time single, my mum, a divorcée, and I, the cute version, were the only constituents at these gatherings. It was before people knew or cared about the fact that you should not give alcohol to children, so there was always wine in the sauce. Maybe this is why I only started drinking well into my adulthood.

Nana learned this pudding from her own grandmother in her childhood, back in Munich, many years before they fled. It must have been truly special, enough to dismiss the cooks from the kitchen, and get down to preparing the shabbat treat themselves. This dish has never been elevated into the state of a recipe. It exists like muscle memory, the way you always head straight to the shops at the slightest sign of a crisis, never unpack your suitcase, and keep all your passports in the everyday backpack, just in case.

When the Nazis came to power, the family sat still for a while, but the Jew-limiting laws of increasing severity came in one after the other a few years later. My teenaged Nana's family council decided that it would be best to flee. And because every other family of wealth went towards the West, the East would be our family's choice. 'Those fools, they all go to America. We go where no one else does!' They did not quite get into the nitty-gritty why, exactly, none of their friends were heading towards Eastern Europe. A classic case of not doing the homework: Hitler's writings were crystal clear in where the pure German living space would be. Well, who can blame them, it was a pretty stomach-churning read, but still a rookie mistake of first-time refugees who let the memory of not-so-distant pogroms pass.

They converted to Christianity, as if the Nazis had not thought of that simple way out, had not immediately ruled such rapid switches as invalid when it came to who was corralled into the ghetto, then onto the cattle train, and then through to the gas chamber. More helpfully, the then beautiful young woman, my grandmother, still rich, found herself a short, ugly, and funny as hell, architect son of middle nobility. This particular combination of historical and hormonal urges did the trick, and they married in record time. Procreational life insurance that separated gorgeous Nana from her siblings, none of whom survived.

Where on earth they were getting all the flour and eggs and milk and butter and cream and sugar and walnuts during the war, escapes me.

The supplies must have come from the family network of Grandpapa, especially after the birth of their first daughter, my aunt, three years into both the war and their marriage. Grandpapa was good at dirty deals. After the war, all the Jewish money was in the Nazis' pockets, and all the noble lands were annexed by a neighbouring country. My grandfather stood there with his young family impoverished but alive, waiting for the Soviet troops to collect him, like all other men of the same rank, to be taken away into the forced labour camps from where the return rate was minimal. Instead, he managed to learn Russian from one day to the next, becoming the favourite translator of the Soviet commander of Budapest, and ended up with an apartment in the most fashionable part of the city in which, incidentally, I was born some twenty-five years later. Being rich is entirely made of acting rich. Well, almost entirely.

III

If you are preparing this dish of domestic pleasure, you should really put together the dough Friday morning, aiming at an afternoon finish, or in my case making it for my new friend, Ömer, Saturday morning, to be ready for his arrival in the evening.

When my daughter Évi turned two years old, we started to make it together, just the two of us. After she woke up from her afternoon sleep, we would put on the table our large ceramic white fruit bowl, so thick-walled it could be used as a construction tool. Into this, we broke the eggs, whatever number we felt like that evening, maybe six, maybe ten, then added milk, sugar, and yeast, mixing them with our hands. Évi loved splashing this mix, and so I kept refilling it, always making the ingredients into a lottery.

This also meant that she built up a tactile idea of the state that the dough needed to achieve. Even today, at sixteen, and as grumpy a teenager as they get, she always comes when I call for the 'human dough machine', grumbling that we might as well use the electric mixer that we have for exactly this purpose. Still, she does it anyway, and to perfection, before slumping back into her dark room of age-appropriate doom.

Why my aunt never learned to make this dish, or my mum, I never figured out. In the transition from wealth to poverty, from live-in maids to decades of Communism's rationed food, from secular German cultural Jewishness to secret, illegal Christianity, fake in both faith and in Hungarianness and yet somehow still managing to be a ticket to stay alive from one day to the next, this tradition skipped a generation.

In the first five years of the war, the Jews were rounded up and taken away to be killed in faraway camps. Brothers, nieces, childhood friends, and grown-up schoolyard bullies, all evaporated into the thin air--a metaphor of the made-up mythology of the übermensch race. The smoke particles spewed out by the chimneys, relentlessly and diligently, spread around in the planet's atmosphere.

It was the last months, October 1944 to February 1945 when the Hungarian Arrow Cross paramilitary started hunting down Jews, not to take them away, but to kill them there and then. The Soviet Union's army was approaching, and these men wanted to finish the job before the inevitable end. In the street where Nana, her husband, and baby daughter lived, those caught were marched down to the river Danube. From the window you could see the men, women and children of all ages, heads down, wearing heavy winter coats and walking slowly to their execution in long queues, armed uniformed men accompanying them. They were lined up and shot at the rim of the water, their bodies floating towards the Black Sea. It was the exact place where I canoed at least a thousand times only three and a half decades later.

Nobody ever, ever, spoke about this. The word 'Jewish' was only whispered by my mother to me, when we were alone, and even then, rarely. Silence was so natural that it never occurred to me that it was weird that she made me swear I would not say it to anyone, let alone Nana, that we were Jews. And I did not.

Even during those days of daily terror, in the immediacy of death, Nana took my two-year-old aunt down for walks in the stroller, so that she could sleep. Some afternoons they would be accidental bystanders to the march of people, desperately careful not to look suspicious when rushing away, but equally careful not to be called out, recognised by friends, and instantly pulled in.

Nana was very disciplined about always having her papers in her pocket. She had a friend with a daughter born the same month, and they timed their baby strolls together, walking and chatting side-by-side. Her friend's papers were real. They'd keep the two sleeping toddlers in the same buggy, pushed by Nana's friend, so that if the Arrow Cross people came with one of those lists of names and addresses of fake Christian Jews, Nana's daughter would survive. This other baby, my aunt's war-twin would become the first female surgeon of Hungary and would operate on me much, much later. A little ankle injury, but she treated me as if I was made of eggshells.

The family that Nana created after the war was poor

and arrogant on the vapour of privilege that had been there only a few years back in calendar time, but which felt like several lifetimes ago. During this time, three sets of friends and family were lost or perished in distinct trauma waves, a recipe for PTSD, the kind that does not jump generations. Only now as I write this have I really thought through what it must have been like to move from Munich, where you grew up, losing people because everyone left, to the corner of five countries in the East. A change from urban cultural elite to countryside gentry, with not only a husband, but having to make completely new social connections. And then a further move, leaving all of these new relationships behind after only four years, just when you were getting established; this time, as a young mother and to the temporary safety of Budapest, where you must again build a brand new life of friends, only to lose them to the Nazis and the war. And all this happened to her in only eight years, from the age of seventeen to twenty-five. No wonder the version of Nana that I knew was mean and infinitely bitter in her Communist-era job of cashier in a hairdressing salon two corners down from her home.

Maybe it is this childhood experience that connects me so strongly to this hands-on dish of love and family warmth, because there was so little of them. And maybe because of this complete dissociation between being rich and elite, and the pulsating presence of the survival threshold that history so frequently brings back in, again and again, that I despise the aristocracy.

IV

I already thought there was something off when Ömer arrived on time, which was classic Oxford passive aggression.

Entirely uncalled for, if you ask me, and aggravated by the fact that he told his date, Colin, to come separately.

We stood a little uncomfortably in the hallway. I was obviously not ready to receive guests, not a naked chef, but almost, and Ömer's eyes were moving between measuring up Alice, assessing the house which we clearly should not be able to afford, and my chest hair.

Finally, I invited him into the kitchen, gave him a glass of wine, and got back to cooking. He did not ask if he could help, just stood there, instantly delving into his lecture about colonialism. How I, with my looks and privilege could never understand historical trauma. All discussion points familiar from our walks. Only the shadowy appearance of my little daughter made him slow down a tad, nevertheless I could barely slip out to put on dinner party clothes.

A polite half an hour later, tank-enthusiast Colin showed up. He was way too sober both for the time of day and for our voyeuristic entertainment of a first date. Thank God that he arrived with Kieran who had definitely fuelled up beforehand. I gave them booze and a bowl of spicy peanuts, freshly roasted, only to find out that Colin was allergic to all three ingredients, which was a curiosity, and a sad one. Who could possibly live without chilli or Sichuan pepper?

When you cook for others, it is—scientifically speaking— giving pleasure. All good chefs are sensual lovers because preparing food is like a sexual act. So if you are good at one skill, you will be good at the other. It is taking pleasure by giving it. We bond with those for whom we cook.

This is why your grandma insisted on you eating more and more. Because she loved you. And it was love she wanted to experience. Every time you had another bite and showed pleasure at it, she experienced a little oxytocin release in her brain. She was the druggie who could not get enough. That natural neuro-peptide oxytocin junkie, Nana, getting high from feeding her beloved grandchild sugary-fatty pleasures.

At least that was my plan for that evening.

I had prepared a goose roast, Lebanese style, culturally appropriated in a particularly sweaty, trying-too-hard way, and still without fireworks. Conversation was dominated by Ömer expounding to Kieran how the historical British vandalism of the planet could never be forgiven, although, he conceded, forgetting might be an option. In return my increasingly drunken Irish friend hit back by detailing the Armenian genocide at the hands of the Ottoman Empire in its last act before collapse. In a twist of debating turns that seemed entirely unintended, he managed to link it to the homophobic nature of the current day Turkish elite. Colin blinked heavily through both subjects, seemingly wishing for an invisibility that went beyond even his everyday ghostly existence.

It was at this point where I reckoned the sugar in the dessert might provide some uplift to the conversation. A bit of fat to cushion the flaring spirits of the room.

Alice and I collected the plates, opened a bottle of sweet bubbly from Alsace, poured it into our set of specially cut crystal glasses, the kind that are only acceptable for marriages, funerals, and listening alone to opera while in a deep depression.

The table had fallen silent by the time I brought out the roasting tin with the bulging brioche shiny with darkened butter, the walnut creating a texture that defies our visual expectations of smoothness. We all put chunks into our bowls. This was china made in Hungary in 1948, and

Grandpapa had acquired it for Nana as a rare luxury. It was gold and blue, a phoenix design, by one of the few Auschwitz survivors who chose to return to Budapest. Still no one spoke as I soaked everyone's nuggets with an egg-yolk and vanilla sauce, with added sweet wine from the region where five countries met, a spot where my family used to own the land 'as far as the eye can see', a saying which I never really believed.

Finally we all took our first bites. A few minutes passed while I wished for the night to end.

'You are only pretending to be Jewish, aren't you...' Ömer suddenly burst out. 'Look at you with your height, blue eyes, blond hair, and German face. Look at you!'

It was as if someone had kicked me in the stomach. The room suddenly became a little hazy, dark. I thought I might throw up. The walls of the room moved around me. My heart seemed to stop beating and I felt my blood pressure drop. Somehow a channel remained open, and I watched the table and the people around it as if from a distance. As if this whole thing was happening to someone else—someone else feeling sick, someone else being violated, someone else who was in danger.

'You are no Jew, are you?' Ömer was staring at me, his brown eyes flashing angrily at something, at someone who must have been there in the room with us.

It was clear that he hated me.

'Are you?' Ömer asked one more time.

Recipe: Tamás's Aranygaluska (Golden Brioche in Hungarian)

A transcription from muscle memory

- First you make a challah dough. For this, mix eggs with milk and sugar and butter and a little salt and yeast. No water, please. You don't ever want to be actually vulgar.
- Make the dough with more kneading than your usual bread, and less flour. It can stay fairly wet. Leave it to rise for a few hours, or overnight. Usual cover-in-thin-layer-of-oil-while-rising rules apply.
- Take a pile of walnuts (making sure that they taste sweet and none of the contaminated bitter taste), and grind half, and break half into small pieces. You should have a bowl of walnuts that are varying in texture and size. Add sugar, tons of grated orange skin (with which you can go all the way tantric, there is never enough), and a little nutmeg, truly just a hint.
- You will need the oven at 180°C/350° F.
- Take a large baking tin, enough for the dough to rise substantially. Melt a ton of butter. (Obviously not an actual ton, but you will need much more than you would expect at first. All European taste bombs are just sugar and butter really with some random spices added.) Take a small piece of the by-now-risen-to-the-peak dough, about the size of a plum, lychee, or lime, depending on which part of the planet you are attempting this from. Dip it entirely into the liquid butter, and then place it in the tin. Make a layer of these. Then put a layer of the orange-peelie walnuts. Then another layer of the buttery nuggets, then another layer of walnuts, and then another layer of the nuggets on the top.

- What is going to happen is that the nuggets will increase in size as they bake, and unevenly, so that the walnut will create a sweet, buttery vein system among the nuggets. Irresistible.
- Bake for about 40-50 minutes. When it looks ready, it usually needs a little more time. You need to make sure that the middle is properly baked, too.
- In the meantime, make a standard crème anglaise—go for the vanilla burst end of the range. If you are not serving it to kids, or adults who do not drink, you can also add white wine—for instance, Tokaji aszú from Hungary, in which case, remember to correct for the sugar when you start off the sauce.
- When ready, serve everyone a bowl of the walnutty aranygaluska (and now you will see why they are golden nuggets) with the sauce poured on top.
- Make sure that all of you go for a very long run the day after. It is not only full of fat and sugar, but it's also impossible to stop eating.

Bon appetit! Jó étvágyat!

Biryani Questions

Jonaki Ray

After she hit me for the eighth time in the eight months that we had been married, I packed up and went back to my parents' home. This time I didn't tell them that it was an argument or that I am coming home for the weekend to give D some space. This time they didn't say, 'Everyone gets angry and overreacts. Let it go.' These words had become an anthem for my life in the last few months. But this time was different. This time they watched silently as I paid the cab, dragged my cases up the porch stairs and into the house, and stowed them in the corner in the living room.

The neighbours finally pulled their curtains back into place, and went back to watching TV again. I knew they would all be calling each other tomorrow, pretending concern, but secretly smirking that their neighbour's son has returned home because his wife beat him. Imagine! 'He is not man enough to keep his wife in check,' they would say. I used to feel my cheeks burning and shame roil my stomach each time I came back and could feel the neighbours' gaze. This time though I turned to Dad and asked about dinner.

'Lentil soup and grilled chicken for me, and I guess, you. Daal-chawal for your Ma. I am just starting, and just so you know, it will take some time before dinner is ready.'

Dad had entered the kitchen only when Ma fell ill. Before that happened, they ruled their separate zones like two rulers of neighbouring kingdoms—Ma, her kitchen, and Dad, his business. In fact, they inhabited different rooms of the house. Ma would be up by 5 a.m., getting breakfast, coffee, and juice ready for Dad and me. She would start the dishes, left overnight in the sink from last night, and vacuum the kitchen every morning, before settling down to her paratha sabzi once Dad and I had left. I would come home after school to find her again in the kitchen, fixing dinner—grilled chicken or fish, soups, salads, and bread— Dad insisted on a continental menu for dinner, even though most of the time he came home too late, too tired, or too wasted to eat anything left on the stove. He never seemed to realise or care that Ma waited for him to eat and go to bed before fixing her own daal-chawal and eating while watching something on TV, and then going to her room to sleep.

I remember asking Ma once, why don't you leave him. This was when she cried for the first time in front of me because he yelled at her for not having dinner ready on time and for not realising how hard he worked to get us a better life.

I had fumed at Ma, 'Does he not realise how much work you put into the house? Why does he act as if you do nothing; as if cooking with hard-to-find ingredients for the recipes that take hours, the hospital-clean house, the weekend parties for neighbours is not work.'

She had wiped her tears, 'I haven't come all the way to a foreign country to break up my family over such a small thing. Besides what will people say? No one would let us live.'

Of course, she had assumed that I would be with her, that she would have to take care of both of us. She had proceeded to say, almost recite, 'A mother always takes care of her duty to her children first, a wife always takes care of her duty to her family first, remember this.'

I don't know what Ma intended by her lectures and monologues about a 'good wife'. What happened instead was that I had ended up wanting a wife who was not like Ma at all. Someone who didn't stay in the kitchen, or wear traditional clothes. When I got married to D, they said I was lucky. Here was someone who was successful, yet grounded. Someone who wanted to marry a man from the home country, but didn't expect to be tied to the kitchen stove or wear a sari, or visit the temple.

'See, she even takes care of the home and is so respectful to her in-laws,' they said. 'And look at the beautiful home that is not within the old quarters pell-mell with the other desis,' they said.

And Ma chanted these words, each time I came home, as if they would be a talisman against my return.

But the mantra didn't work because what happened inside our home was a replay of D's parents, except that she was her father, and I was her mother. The first time she hit me, even my hand had lifted. She had, in fact, told me the second time that if I wanted, I could hit her and get my anger out of the system. But my parents' marriage, with all its flaws, had never been one where they hit each other. And so I stopped myself. I did tell D that I am not going to accept this, and left for my parents' place. Each time, after a day or two, D would message or call, and the last two times, even came to pick me up. She would apologise and then for a few days it would be like our honeymoon—amazing sex, takeaway food and snuggling together at night, telling each other stories from our daily lives and the highlights of our past. And then, D would come home after a tough day at work and start yelling at me for watching TV and ignoring her. Or I would be late home and that would tick her off. Nothing I did would be right for her—even the Sundays that I went home to my parents would cause her to yell, throw things around, and the last couple of times, pull my hair, slap, and punch me. She would turn into an entirely different person, like a female version of Jekyll and Hyde, and the cycle would begin again.

I always believed each time she would stick to her words and not hit me again.

I didn't want to tell anyone what had happened, though I knew that people were gossiping. Our neighbours and friends had heard the shouts and seen my bruises. And the news spread like chai boiling over, spilling all over the stove. I never told my parents though—I was too ashamed, and they never asked me. And I always went back to D. I felt that I had to be the good guy, the one who had to make sure not to trigger her in some way. And I hoped that things would change. After all, I had seen my parents' marriage become better with time.

Over the years, Dad became a calmer person once he sold off his business and started writing about his travels. He stopped drinking so much—at the most, a glass of wine with his dinner, Ma confided. Once he was home more, he realised that Ma held the family together. Besides, he could no longer pull the 'I'm making the money and what do you contribute' question. Ma had gone back to college by then, finished her degree in business, and started a catering business with two of her college friends. She ignored the neighbours when they said, '*boodhi ghodi lal lagaam*, look at the old horse putting on a red bridle.'

Every time I came home, I could see the change in the routine at home as well. Dad had started getting up early, making tea for Ma, fixing breakfast—simple stuff like oatmeal and fruit, but still, a change from the past. Ma would leave for her classes and study groups, wearing Western outfits—fitted blazers and pantsuits, matched with jaunty scarfs. Dad would vacuum the house, then fix himself a sandwich (and one for me during the few days I retreated to their place), and sit in his study writing his blogs until sunset. Every evening he would then start a soup and salad for himself, and daal or rajma-chawal for Ma's dinner. He changed from wearing a business suit every day to wearing T-shirts and shorts. Ma, who had always been conscious about her English, had started speaking more confidently, and they went out for coffees and dinner dates, often leaving me alone at home. They had even started sharing a room, though I didn't want to think too much about what happened behind that door!

Today though, when I go to sit next to her, Ma turns her head, her scalp visible against the thinning hair, and doesn't talk about Dad or any evening plans. She has only two more chemo rounds, and tells me that the doctor is positive about the prognosis.

'I know I am going to beat this,' she says in a low voice, as if she's exhausted of telling herself this many times. She is wearing an old housecoat that seems to drain all the colour and energy from her, but smiles at me, 'It's good to have you back home.' When Dad clears his throat, 'Well, it's time for me to head to the kitchen and fix dinner', she turns to him and says, 'Why don't we have chicken biryani today? All of us together?'

There is a pause, and then both Dad and I say, 'Of course!' and get up to go to the kitchen simultaneously.

In the kitchen, Dad starts laying out the spices—cinnamon, bay leaf, cloves, cardamom, red chillies, black pepper, saffron—and tells me, 'Why don't you wash the rice and let it soak?'

'I know, Dad. I was the one who used to make the biryani for special occasions, remember?'

The rice is washed and soaked in water—just enough to cover it—in a bowl. Dad starts pounding the spices and marinating the chicken in a bowl of yoghurt. I take out three onions and prepare to cut them into fine, long slices. Ma has come into the kitchen as well and is sitting in the blue chair that is placed next to the backyard window that always catches the last of the sunshine.

The kitchen is full of the smell of spices and raw onions when Ma asks, 'Sonu, does she hit you?'

I watch the tears fall onto the cutting board as I say, 'Yes.'

Recipe: Basic One-Pot Chicken Biryani

Ingredients:

1 bay leaf
2-3 cloves
2-3 cardamom
1 tsp red chilli
1 tsp cumin
1-2 sticks of cinnamon

1 tbsp garam masala
½ cup of ginger and garlic minced and blended into a
    paste
1-2 onions cut into fine slices
1 or 2 tbsp ghee
½ kg chicken cut into pieces
1 cup basmati rice
½ cup yoghurt

Method:

- Marinate the chicken in a bowl of yoghurt, ginger-garlic paste and garam masala for about 30 minutes, or 1 hour, depending on how much time you have.
- Wash and soak a cup of rice for about 30 minutes.
- Sauté the spices in ghee. Add the onions and fry till soft.
- Add the marinated chicken and fry for 2 to 5 minutes.
- Put the lid on the pot, or pressure cook and let it cook for two whistles.
- Take a broad dish and layer with the chicken.
- Add the rice on top and add two cups of water.
- Put the lid on and let it cook for around 10 to 12 minutes, or pressure cook for two whistles.

Catastrophe

Uttaran Das Gupta

'You call us home for lunch, but you give us only drunch!'
It is Promila shouting down into the stairwell from the
door of the roof. Utsav and Banalata are on the landing
right below.

'What's drunch?' Utsav cries back.

'It's lunch, but so late that it's become dinner.'

The cadence of her voice can accommodate playfulness
with authority: 'Stop making out both of you and come up.'

Promila withdraws to the roof, where she is skewering
kebabs, with help from all their other friends. The smoke
from the smouldering coals rises in irregular wisps towards
a smoggy January sky.

Utsav had come down to the flat to pick up a few bottles
of beer. On his way back, Banalata cornered him.

'Do you like your birthday party?' she demands, kissing
him.

She is the organiser and host of the celebration; it is
taking place on the roof of the building, where she and
another girl rent the top-floor flat. Utsav is a not infrequent,
overnight guest.

In response to her question, he puts his mouth on hers.
When they part, she asks again: 'Well?'

'Yes, of course.'

'So what are you going to give me?'

He pauses for only a moment before replying: 'More sex!'

She laughs, throwing her head back. 'You would like that, wouldn't you?'

They quickly climb the stairs, their fingertips almost touching. But as they step on to the roof, a vortex opens up for Utsav. Despite being drunk, he knows that his birthday will always provoke memories of the catastrophe.

***

It occurred almost half a lifetime ago. The incident was a minor one and should have been deleted from memory; for some inexplicable reason it had lingered on like an undetected hairline fracture on his ribs.

Utsav did not have too many birthday parties while growing up. You can't really invite your friends from an upscale Catholic missionary school to your home if you live in a one-room tenement with an asbestos roof. It was not in the slums, but almost. They had lived there for three years from the time Utsav was about seven years old.

The grey zone of distance and proximity allowed his family—father, mother, sister, and him—to cling on to the promontory of respectability with their fingertips. This was not really a shelter from the elements. When it rained, the roof rang out with the rat-a-tat of a machine gun. On summer afternoons, the room was like the inside of an oven, the air too hot to breathe, the ceiling fan impotent. At dusk, their mother would make Utsav and his sister take baths, put on fresh clothes, loads of talcum powder, and they would walk to Southern Avenue. The tree-lined road that girdled the Lake was about ten minutes away.

It was cool there. On one side of the road were multi-storeyed buildings, all facing south. Utsav's mother told them that these were windswept on stuffy, humid evenings. Utsav once spotted a Mercedes near the Kali temple.

'Will we ever live here?' they would ask her.

'So many houses,' she would reply. 'I am sure there would be space in at least one of them for us.'

But not yet. Not yet. After the walk, they sometimes had phuchka, before returning to their home with the asbestos roof.

If someone wanted to break in at night, it would not have been too difficult. The door was only two planks of wood in a weak frame. It was bolted every night to assuage the anxieties of the people inside, just enough for them to sleep. But anyone could have kicked it in if they wanted. Perhaps the only thing that kept criminals away was the evident poverty of the house. What could it have that was worth their time?

Things were incredibly hard in those days. The mongrel of poverty gnawed constantly at the door. Utsav's parents usually got the monthly rations from the local mudi shop on credit and would at times be unable to pay back the next month. There was always some extra expense—maybe some friend's wedding, some school project that needed an extra hundred rupees. They ran out of food once and the mudi shop owner refused to extend any credit. Utsav could not recall later how this matter was sorted but perhaps some benevolent relative came to their rescue.

The nocturnal ritual of bolting the door did not always ensure a complete exorcism of anxieties. For instance, the night on which the Calcutta Municipal Corporation and the police decided to evict the hawkers who had encroached upon both sides of the arterial Rash Behari Avenue. They listened to the sirens and bulldozers till daybreak. When their father took them out in the morning for the school bus, they saw the remains of the itinerant shops of refugees that had been reduced to rubble. Their father had picked up a small flag of the Marxist party, the overfamiliar hammer and sickle on the red background, which had fallen on the road. He had once been a member of its more radical wing.

The school bus dropped him back every afternoon on Rash Behari Avenue. One could not spot their tenement from the road. This was a good thing. He had shown another building with yellow ochre walls to his friends and told them he lived there. Utsav, of course, did not know the inmates of that house, besides an ill-tempered cocker spaniel that barked at him and his sister whenever they went past it. That is how all these large houses were. On the wall outside, there would usually be a marble plaque with the names of the owners and their academic qualifications acquired in Britain, the odour of dog piss near the gates.

Where had he acquired this habit of giving out a false address? Probably from his father, who had provided the details of their older house at Gariahat as residential data to both Utsav's and his sister's schools. It was an almost harmless falsehood, born out of aspiration perhaps. Who could blame him for dreaming of a better life? It was also a desire—to return. Utsav's father had been born in that house, had grown up there. He had learnt to navigate the city by making that his axis. Utsav and his sister were also born in that house. To be ejected from it was as much a loss for him as it had been for his ancestors migrating from

Jessore at the time of Partition. The exact conditions under which they had been ejected were not clear to Utsav. His uncle—his father's elder brother—still lived there, with his family. They visited sometimes.

It was in the Gariahat house that Utsav had his last proper birthday party. Or at least that is what the photographs provided evidence for, because he could not remember it at all. He was four years old then and went to a primary school. All his friends and cousins had been invited and his mother had made chilli chicken and fried rice. One of his uncles got slightly drunk and sang 'Happy Birthday' a little overenthusiastically.

The high point of that party was the chocolate-flavoured cake, shaped like a steam engine. It had been made to order at Kathleen, the confectionary shop near Cornfield Road. 'It was so good that it melted in your mouth,' his mother would tell them later.

Since they had moved to the house with the asbestos roof, the only cakes that had come for Utsav's or his sister's birthdays were from the nearest Monginis shop. These were readymade—usually round, sometimes rectangular. The icing was often oversweet and refused to dissolve on your tongue; at times you had to down several glasses of water to ease a slice through your gullet.

Yes, they still celebrated birthdays, though, as we said earlier, none of his friends from school were invited. The guests were mostly his mother's relatives—her mother, her brother, his wife, their children. Utsav and his sister were both January-born, so they would often have one evening of celebrations rather than two. A convenient strategy to economise.

These occasions might not have much glitter, but they

were not wholly devoid of joy either. Food was usually cooked at home, his mother slaving away for hours in the lightless room that served as their kitchen. Neither Utsav nor his sister liked payesh, the rice pudding that was a staple on such occasions, so she made carrot halwa, grating the vegetables finely and then torturing them in milk and sugar. She was a little superstitious about this.

'The milk should never curdle,' she told her children, 'that's a bad omen.'

Who needs confirmation for a year of bad luck on their birthday?

One year, Utsav's father bought him a Moby Books edition of *The Adventures of Huckleberry Finn*. The price of these books was no more than thirty or thirty-five rupees. At first, Utsav was a little disappointed as he had expected a set of sketch pens or a GI Joe toy. When he finished the book, however, he wondered if he would ever be able to write something like this.

They had just started using fountain pens in school. Utsav had an olive-green Wing Sung that he treasured as if it were something more than a cheap writing instrument. Filling it up with Chelpark Royal Blue, he embarked upon a downstream adventure like Huck and Jim. The endeavour was a poor imitation of the original, and he gave up soon, realising that navigating a raft down the Mississippi of narrative was not a boys' task.

Where did they get the money for these gifts, these celebrations? Utsav would realise later that most of their family expenses were borne out of the charity of relatives. Or, by selling the meagre amount of gold jewellery that his mother had got at her wedding. It was precious little: a couple of necklaces, rings studded with semi-precious stones, earrings, a silver spoon he got at his first rice ceremony, a platinum watch on a bob chain that had long ceased to be an effective timekeeper but definitely had some resale value. All this was stored in a bank locker. By the middle of each month, his father's salary would run out. If appeals to her brothers' generosity failed to yield any results, Utsav's mother would make the inevitable trip to the bank to extract a sufficient artefact, and then to a pawnbroker to sell it off. This is how the mudi shop had been paid off.

Utsav had accompanied her several times on these pilgrimages. After the pawnbroker, his mother would usually go to the fish market at Gariahat. One might as well have one good dinner a month if they were selling off their gold.

This was a confusing place for a child. The sellers hollered their discounts and the freshness of their wares to attract buyers; the humid air would be thick with the stench of aquatic life; light bulbs descended like fruit from the ceiling, hanging by electric wires. A cat could usually be seen perched on the nook of a high wall, calculating when it could slip down and steal the fish.

***

When Banalata first proposed celebrating his birthday, Utsav demurred. 'But why not?' she asks.

'I don't really like it,' he says.

'Who doesn't like their birthday?'

Utsav reluctantly tells her his reasons. 'You know, when we were children, Ma had to borrow money from her brothers, our mamas, for our birthdays.'

She kisses him on the cheek. 'That's in the past, no?'

she says in a kind voice. 'We don't have to borrow anything from anyone to have a few friends over for lunch.'

There is no way to counter this line of reasoning, so he capitulates. Little does he know then about the hairline fracture, the vortex.

***

After three years—the usual length of a lease contract in Calcutta—in the house with the asbestos roof, it was time for them to find a new home. Also, his sister was a little older now, and their mother said it was not safe. A broker was consulted, and new accommodation was found. This was a more permanent structure—the ground floor of a two-storeyed building. The owner's family lived on the first floor. Though not really comfortable by any means, this was an enormous improvement to their conditions. This flat had two rooms, the larger one serving as their bedroom, while the smaller one was kitchen, drawing room, dining room, Utsav's study et al. This was a little further from the slums, a little closer to bourgeois comforts.

(Several years later, at university, Utsav would be very surprised to find many of his Left-minded friends, who had grown up ensconced in these comforts, critical of the same. They often threatened to abjure such a life and go join the rebels at Jangalmahal. Of course, none of them actually did it; their parents took them to Europe for summer holidays.)

On their first night in this new house, they had a simple dinner of rice, daal and boiled potatoes. The air was humid with relief and satisfaction. Utsav's mother had a confession to make: 'Whenever I would see these houses, I would pray to God that surely there was a home for us in one of these.'

It was perhaps this sense of relief that made them less vigilant, that allowed for the catastrophe.

This is how it occurred.

Utsav's classmate Sayan invited him for a birthday party. This was new and strange. If you did not ask people to your house, they would not ask you to theirs—that was the rule. Utsav's parents did not really know how to deal with this situation. Since Sayan's house was not very far away, they agreed to let him go. A gift was acquired and wrapped up in shiny paper, and he was dropped off at the address on the invitation card. It was a seventh-floor flat of a multi-storeyed building on Southern Avenue. It faced the Lake and was windswept, like they had always imagined.

Sayan's father was a doctor; he had some taste in art and literature and had done up his flat aesthetically. The furniture was polished teak, well-rounded and with no hurtful edges; the curtains were brown and thick; the carpets were so soft that your feet sank in them; the lights were muted and yellow, not the harsh white tube lights in Utsav's house. They had two servants who served dinner on heavy China plates and it was eaten with cutlery that shone like glass. Sayan even had a desktop computer with the latest version of Prince of Persia, and he let his friends try it out. Some of them were pretty good at it; Utsav was not. The only computers he had access to were the ones during class hours in school.

After the party at Sayan's house, Utsav was invited to several others. It was as if his schoolmates had conducted an audition and found him good enough to be admitted into their tribe. He, too, took full advantage of this opportunity, familiarising himself with the social rituals expected of him with alacrity, playing his part at these occasions without a false note. This was dangerous as he would soon find out.

Utsav did not know another rule of these tribal engagements: you cannot keep accepting invitations and not extend any. His parents, of course, did, so a few weeks before his next birthday, they said to him: 'Why don't you call a few of your friends?'

This proposition was something new, exciting. Later, much later, any development which provoked such feelings would inspire in him a great distrust, even fear of disaster. But then, he was too young and untrained, and he allowed himself to be carried away by the currents, unaware of where they would take him.

The guest list wasn't too long; the size of their flat ensured it. Three people were invited: Sayan, of course, and Rahul and his younger brother Rohan. There were others who had been considered but what tilted the scales in the favour of these three was that Rahul had invited Utsav's sister to his birthday party the previous year. The brothers studied in Utsav's school, but they were not Bengali or even from Calcutta. Their father was a manager in the branch of one of the many South Indian banks that did business in the city.

On the morning of his party, Utsav was filled with an unfamiliar anticipation, manifesting itself in a shortness of breath. By the time his friends arrived in the afternoon, it had retreated to a sort of dullness behind his ribs.

The party began on a bit of a false note. Utsav's mother served the guests Thums Up and potato chips, but Sayan refused to have the cold drink.

'My father says Thums Up corrodes your teeth,' he declared. 'You can actually use it to clean your toilet. It will be all shiny.'

The glasses of cola stood untouched, losing carbon

dioxide. Utsav's friends sat around on low stools, munching chips. They looked uncomfortable. The room, which had seemed large enough to accommodate all of them, seemed to have shrunk, the knees of the guests touching as they sat around the table. Utsav did not have any computer games to entertain his friends, and there were not enough of them to play 'Mafia' or 'Killer'.

Finally, lunch was served.

Sayan took one look at the bowls of chicken and fried rice and said to Utsav's mother: 'Have you made anything vegetarian? Rahul and Rohan don't eat chicken.'

This was an almost casual declaration; to Utsav's ears, it was like a thunderclap.

Utsav's mother turned to him. 'You didn't tell me they were vegetarian,' she said.

'I didn't know.' Utsav felt as helpless as a convict about to mount the gallows.

'Didn't you ask them?'

'No.'

'Why?'

'I didn't know.'

'You always have to ask your guests about their food preference. Don't you know?'

Utsav did not know. Was this knowledge somehow accessible to everyone? If it was, how did he not know?

He stood there almost paralysed, but his parents had swung into action. His father went out quickly to get paneer. His mother prepared the curry in the meanwhile. Lunch was inevitably delayed, but not long enough to be called drunch. He did not know the word then.

After the meal, Sayan proposed that they go to his house. His driver and car were waiting, and they could play Prince of Persia. Rahul agreed immediately. Utsav saw his friends off till the car and then walked back home reluctantly. His mother, exhausted with the day's labour, was watching TV. His father had dozed off.

Utsav sat down at his study table and looked at the book Sayan had gifted him. It was *The Lost World* by Sir Arthur Conan Doyle. It would be evening soon, and a swarm of mosquitoes would descend on the city like an invading army. He did not tell anyone, but a dull ache was starting in his ribs.

This was not an ache he could put his finger on. Utsav would carry it around with him, to other houses in the city, to Delhi and Berlin, to London and Prague. And, he would almost forget about it, except when the vortex opened.

Recipe: Pork Curry

Ingredients:

1 kg pork (with fat and bones)
½ kg onions
¼ kg garlic
¼ kg ginger
1 small cup dark rum
2 level tsp salt
½ tsp sugar
1 heaped tsp turmeric powder
1 level tsp red chilli powder
2 tsp coriander powder
2 tsp cumin powder

Method:

- Clean the pork and cook in a pressure cooker. The number of whistles required varies on the size of the utensil, but I usually go for 5 or 6. (You can use a saucepan with a lid as well; it will just take longer to get tender.)

- Add finely chopped onions, ginger and garlic.
- Add all sugar and salt, along with the spices. Last, add the dark rum.
- Cook again for 5 or 6 whistles in the pressure cooker. Check that the meat is fully cooked. You will know it is when you can separate the meat from the bone with a fork. Serve with rice.

Note: As this is a spicy dish, it is best to have a green salad to go with it.

Of Loss and Desserts

Paresh Tiwari

I am in the study, attempting to read when he calls. I hear the phone—an innocuous buzz that quickly turns insistent. It bleeds over the strains of 'The Carnival of Animals' playing on the music box. I like to read with this one composition playing on the loop, swirling around me like the perfume of a lover's skin. It's perfect for an afternoon of lazy reading, though there's nothing lazy about it today. I watch the phone from the corner of my eye. Barely five feet away, dancing about the polished wood of the coffee table, the face lit up, a small green icon hopping around the screen, begging me to swipe it up. But when I decide to give in and uncoil my feet, stretch them on the cold floor to step over and pick up the call, the phone gives up. He gives up. The silence is unnerving. And it takes a moment or two before the music swells up and reclaims the room. The phone screen stays lit for a while, almost like the bitter aftertaste of stale coffee. It is in those moments that I make the decision. Switching on my laptop, I search for flights to Mumbai.

He had called last evening when I was in the kitchen. And though it wasn't a number I recognised, I'd accepted the call, all the while stirring curry, breathing in the aroma of ginger and garlic, lifting up the ladle to taste for saltiness.

'You don't know me,' came a man's voice out of the blue, 'but I would like to take ten minutes of your time.'

'Of course, I don't,' I blurted back in surprise and then added, 'How do you know me?'

'I don't,' he said, 'not personally, though I know about you from someone we both love.'

'There are very few people I love,' I ended up saying before I could filter it out. 'Is this some sort of a prank call? Did someone put you up to this?'

'It's a delicate matter, Namrata,' he said, ignoring my question completely, 'not really suited for a phone call.'

By now, I was hooked. His voice instilled a sense of trust. Some voices creep you out, and then there are those squarely on the opposite end of the spectrum. One could even assign it a colour—almost amber—as if the voice oozed warmth. I turned the stove off. Placed a lid over the pot of simmering curry and shifted the phone to my right hand.

'Okay, go on. You have my attention,' I said, 'but let's start with introductions.'

'If it matters,' he paused, 'my name is Tahaan. Malik.' He took too many pauses, as if thinking on his feet. 'I have been hearing about you for one and a half decades now. I'd like to think that I know you.'

That was unbelievable. Even I didn't remember who I was fifteen years ago.

'Sometimes I feel that all we ever did was talk about you.'

'Who is this we?'

'Why did you stop painting?' He flung another question at me in response.

I was definitely not enjoying this line of dialogue. It

had begun to make me feel vulnerable, as if the voice was somehow undressing me, peeling off layers of existence from my flesh.

'Did you know they cut down the banyan tree six years ago?'

It's strange how the mind behaves when faced with something it isn't expecting. Looking back now at the conversation, I realise that I should have been worried. I should have disconnected the call and dialled the police. But I didn't. Instead, I walked over to the window and drew the curtains to one side. I looked at the Ganges and the tall trees by its bank, a couple of hundred meters away. And beyond that, the mountain peaks reaching up for the sky. I remembered thinking, would there ever be a tree with a cooler shade than my childhood banyan. It was like a friend and I had trusted it with so many secrets—the old tin box stuffed with stumps of crayons and coins and postcards—I had believed were safe there. Perhaps they are safer now. Tahaan's voice had receded to a background drone. I vaguely remember words that must have held meaning and must have been strung together to form a coherent narrative. But I can't be sure. I believe he said something about reading all of my books. And about the absurdity of living in a large city where one couldn't even walk without jostling for the little space that is every human's right, whether living or dead. I think he also spoke about the weather and the impending rains. But it wasn't until he mentioned her name that I truly heard him.

'She died last night,' he said as if it were the most natural thing in the world to say.

***

Her hair was a silver waterfall gurgling over the soft hills of her shoulders. The first time I had seen her, I had wondered how she still had a full head, unlike Ma, whose hair had thinned out, parting centre first, like the ocean after manthan, the churning. It was the day Nana died. It was also the day my first tooth fell out. As the mourners filed in one by one, I stood twirling the blue lace curtains in my fingers, sucking the embroidered half-moon, the five-petal flower, the crooked leaf, and the butterfly in flight. I tasted them all, one by one, until the tooth dislodged. It wasn't a spindly bottom tooth like most kids lose first, but a fat top front one. I rolled it around under my tongue, fingered the hole in my mouth, and then eased the still-flecked-with-blood tooth into my cupped palm.

As the mourners' wails grew louder, and Nana was borne away on drooping shoulders, I wove through the maze of bare brown feet and white fabric. Snatches of conversations pitter-pattered over my ears, '…what will become of her?' '…alone at this age? What choice does she have? Daughter's home?…Tch. Tch. Tch.' I reached Nani and held out my hand. She was looking straight ahead, her chin held up high. It took her a moment to realise what I was trying to show her. The tooth lay in the middle of my palm, a corn kernel, its enamel shining white under the fluorescent tubelights. Nani pulled on the edge of the purple sari covering her head, and it's then that I got a glimpse of her hair. She picked up the tooth and folded it into her fist.

Fourteen days later, after the last rites had all been completed, I helped her pack the suitcase. Petticoats, blouses, salwar-kameez sets, a pashmina shawl and two soft towels were folded into rectangles and placed at the bottom. Then came a small silver paandaan, a photo album, and a soiled leather-bound copy of *Summer in Calcutta*. Brightly coloured saris—peacock green, vermillion, yellow, royal blue—an abridged rainbow made up the topmost layer. The underclothes were rolled and stuffed in the corners. None of Nana's stuff made it to the suitcase, not even the photo on the bedside table.

'You can't take everyone on every journey, Nimmo,' Nani said, stepping back to look at the bulging luggage. I hitched my skirt up to the knees and sat on top of the lid to help Papa click the locks in place.

In Bangalore, a room in the southern corner of the three-bedroom flat was prepared for her. The floor was covered with a rug, and a metal almirah was shifted from my room to hers. A study table and a chair were placed next to the window that opened to the old banyan resting on a hundred limbs. Nani refused to unpack despite Ma's repeated entreaties. 'It's just for a while,' she said. 'I tend to forget how I hate permanence. I want to remember it this time.' The paandaan and the book, however, were pulled out and placed on the table.

After dinner, I settled down on Nani's bed.

'First tooth calls for a celebration, doesn't it, Nimmo?' Nani said, taking out a betel leaf from the paandaan. With a flick of her wrist, she applied a thin layer of lime and catechu paste over the leaf, placed three betel nuts in the centre, rolled it into a small cone, and put it in her mouth, 'Let's do something fun tomorrow.'

The next afternoon, when I returned from school, I found Nani in the kitchen. Her hair was rolled into a bun and she was in a bright yellow sari. An old forgotten radio was playing songs that I had never heard before. They sounded nimble as if someone had freed them from the responsibility of bearing the burden of an entire orchestra. 'Break the seviyan into palm-length pieces,' Nani instructed, chopping dry fruits into a bowl. She lit the stove, placed a pan over it and added a dollop of ghee. Into the gently sizzling ghee she stirred the seviyan, the strands of vermicelli, till they turned the colour of my palms and the kitchen erupted with a rich golden aroma. She then added milk, sugar and cardamom powder to the dessert. 'Will you run to my room and bring the book?' she said, taking the pan off the heat and pouring the contents into a large glass dish.

When I brought her the book, she flipped through the pages and extracted a folded sheet of butter paper. 'This is called waraq, Nimmo,' she said, revealing a thin rectangle as silver as her own hair and as brittle as moonlight. 'You know how it is made? It is born of dancing wrists, tuk-tuk-tuk. Tuk-tuk-tuk,' she said, clucking her tongue, 'that and an ounce of silver beaten to death between two pieces of cowhide.' Nani's eyes lit up as she spread the waraq over the dessert, tapping it gently into place.

'Even kimami seviyan needs the touch of death to shine,' she said with a flourish. 'What do you say, is it a gift fit enough for the first tooth?'

***

Nani had been staying with us for almost two months now. We had unpacked most of her stuff. During this time, we had shared bedtime stories, sung songs, and even painted together. I had learnt the names of all the flowers that grew in our compound. Sometimes I brought some of the brighter ones so she could wear them in her braid. One night after dinner, Nani pulled out the album from her suitcase and flipped it open on the bed. I turned the browning sheets one by one by one. The bright eyes and the conspiratorial smile in the photographs were instantly recognisable. Whether she was standing with her back to a mountain or on the beach, whether she was sitting at her study table or in a train compartment, she smiled as if she knew a secret that she just might tell you if you came a little closer. It was, however, her photograph next to a lemon tree that caught my eye.

'Curls were all the rage, Nimmo,' she said, 'It took me a week to get them right.'

'Nani, you look so pretty.'

Nani tipped her head back and gave a throaty laugh. 'That's the way life is, the worth of things is seen only in hindsight. But then you realise that this road has no U-turn.'

The next day she packed her suitcase again. Everything except the saris went back in. 'They will make chic skirts,' she winked at me, as Papa rolled the suitcase out of the main gate into the cavernous belly of the taxi.

I don't even remember all the nights the eight-year-old me waited for Nani to return wheeling her fancy suitcase. All the days I tried to remember the words to the songs we had sung together. Over the years, her name became taboo. There were times when Ma and Papa would stop talking when I entered the room, but I could intuitively tell it was about her. '…at this age? I couldn't even face Mrs Sharma at the kitty party today. He is around your age…Is that why she turned away from her own family?'

***

I land at Mumbai airport early in the morning on a runway still glazed with rain. My eyes follow the landing lights, the guide markings, and the many-hued footwear till the air curtains at the exit gates slice through my haze and deposit me onto moist grey streets. That's where I meet Tahaan for the first time. I see a tall man with a short-cropped greying beard dressed in pale blue denims, a white kurta, and flip-flops. He takes my duffel bag, despite the cloth satchel flung over his left shoulder and we walk over to a waiting Uber.

'I can't drive in this city,' he says, settling down in the back seat to my right, 'I have spent close to twenty years here and I still can't wrap my head around it.'

'Why didn't you call me earlier? When she was alive?'

'She didn't want that,' he says with a finality that stops me from asking any more questions.

The taxi weaves in and out of the traffic, honking its displeasure at the sluggish cars and bikes, until we reach the Bandra-Worli Sea Link. It's a snaking bridge suspended over the ocean's swell, held together with the kind of dichotomy only Mumbai is capable of. To my left, just below the bridge, I can make out small shanties and machua (fisherman) boats moored over mounds of tetra-pods. To my right, glass and brick buildings squint at the sun peeking through the clouds.

'She was adamant that only you be told of her death,' he says, picking up the threads of the conversation again, 'I know she wanted to see you. It's beyond me why she didn't. Perhaps she wanted you to remember her the way she imagined you do.'

'But I don't. Not much anyway. She didn't have the right to expect anything,' I say, seething with something that I am unable to identify.

Tahaan nods as if coming to terms with this statement. The taxi eases by Marine Lines station. There are vegetable vendors displaying their wares on the road and people haggling with them, ignoring the honking cars and bikes. There's calm in this chaos and I feel my breath gaining its rhythm back. And then we stop in front of a large iron gate painted a curious shade of blue.

The guard at the gate looks at us with tired eyes, before recognition flashes. He leaps up from his stool and bows, 'As-salamu alaykum, janaab.'

'Wa' alaykumu s-salam, Ahmed,' Tahaan responds, 'everything all right?'

'By the grace of Allah.'

'Peace be upon Him,' Tahaan continues, 'may we visit the departed?'

The gate swings open on squeaking hinges and we enter the cemetery. I follow Tahaan barefoot amid the overgrown weeds, the flowering trees, the still wet grass, a dozen frangipani scattered about, and the half-obliterated epitaphs in calligraphic Urdu, until we reach the fresh mound of earth that is supposed be her.

'You probably need to eat something,' Tahaan says after we leave the cemetery, 'there's a place that I think you will like.'

The bakery is a short walk from the cemetery. The man behind the counter smiles and nods at us as we take one of the two tables inside. Without a word he brings two plates with slices of mawa cake over to our table.

'Chai?' He is a master at the art of minimal conversation.

'Yes, please.' Tahaan smiles at him.

'Try it,' he nudges me, 'it's Ahalya's recipe.'

He says her name as if it were a prayer rolling down his tongue. I take a bite of the cake and I am suddenly hungry. The cake is warm and sweet. It's like I had never had a slice of cake before. I eat three of the slices, which seems to please Tahaan inordinately. Between sips of hot tea, he starts to talk, and I listen as he speaks of the time he met her at this very bakery, and how he had come back—not for the rolls or the bread—but to speak to her.

'She had spent her life conforming to the idea of who she was supposed to be for everyone,' he says, 'until she decided to find herself. She found herself in this city, in this bakery. In the ovens full and empty. Her life was beaded together with little rebellions and yet she was scared of being judged by those she loved most.'

'I wouldn't have judged her.'

'Maybe not. And I think she knew that. She took time to see it, she eventually did. By then though, things had changed, we had found out about the lumps branching in her lungs.' He slides the battered copy of *Summer in Calcutta* over the table.

I flip open the pages to find a rectangular piece of waraq folded between two sheets of paper, a sheet of paper that I open to see is the recipe of kimami seviyan, and a photograph. A shrunken Nani, looking back at me, her hair, the silver waterfall that I remember caressing her shoulders, all gone. Her head is a moon reflecting the glaze of the sun, but her eyes are still bright, and a conspiratorial smile is creeping from the corner of her lips as if she knows a secret that she just might tell you if you come a little closer. I close the book and slip it into the pocket of my vermillion silk waistcoat.

RECIPE: SCRAMBLED EGGS

(Paresh's favourite egg preparation)

Ingredients for 2 servings:

4 eggs
¼ cup cold milk
2 tsp butter
Salt
Pepper

Method:

- Beat eggs and milk in a medium bowl until blended.
- Heat butter in a large non-stick skillet over medium heat until hot. Pour in the egg mixture.
- As eggs begin to set, gently pull the eggs across the pan with a spatula, forming large soft clouds.
- Continue cooking, all the while pulling, lifting and folding the eggs. Once the mixture begins to thicken, remove from heat and continue to cook over the remnant heat of the skillet until no visible liquid egg remains.
- Serve with salt and pepper to taste.
- Spice up this recipe by adding Pepper Jack and salsa on the side. For a breakfast fit for kings, serve with crispy fried bacon, toast, butter and marmalade.

The Honeymoon

Nusrat Durrani

I

On the drive from JFK to Brooklyn in the aluminium twilight, Gulrang leaned against the window of the yellow taxi. Arsalan reached for her hand and squeezed, traffic slowly passing a construction site under the aqueduct. Gul was tired from the sixteen-hour flight but smiled her crooked smile and the lights of the highway danced across her face like a string of yellow pearls. For a moment, in the tungsten shadows, she looked like Asmahan, the Egyptian singer from the fifties—an ungodly beauty with luscious lips and hypnotic eyes, rumoured to be a spy, who died young in a mysterious car accident.

Five years of courtship, three years of marriage, and Arsalan was still in love with Gul, enslaved to her famous gorgeousness. She was an enlightened woman, one of the country's best doctors, and according to the grapevine, being groomed to be the next minister for health. No one had done more for women and children in the nation. Arsalan knew he was a lucky man.

The honeymoon they had promised each other since forever had begun—eight weeks of uninterrupted pleasure, in the world's most exciting and decadent city. When they met late one night, in line for falafel at Mamoun's, they were two outcasts from a country with a weird name most people didn't know. The city hammered them into shape: they hustled their way through college, got lucky, got fucked-up, lived the twisted poetry of life as foreign students in Manhattan, and became the unlikely ambassadors of their tiny kingdom. Gul was an only child whose widowed mother invested her life savings in her daughter's education at New York University's Medical Center. Tough but exhilarating years for both of them. Arsalan was an MFA student at Columbia at the time. 'My son attended the same university as Obama,' his father never failed to mention at family gatherings. Arsalan wanted to become famous like Jack Kerouac or Hunter Thompson, or J.D. Salinger, all Columbia alma mater.

The university rejected his application thrice and by the time his acceptance letter arrived, he had seen so much shit in life, and his head was already so warped, he didn't think he needed Columbia University to write a book. He fled to New York anyway. Who wouldn't? It was a place for nonconformists, black magic, and myths. He would fit right in. Never in his wildest dreams did he think he would one day be writing the definitive modern history of his misunderstood place of birth. One commissioned by His Royal Highness himself. A narrative to set the record straight once and for all, to restore honour and dignity of a kingdom maligned in the West for its bloody rebellions, palace intrigues, wealth and abject poverty.

'Which country you from?' the taxi driver asked. The man was wearing a surgical mask. When Arsalan answered, the driver replied 'Never heard of it, but at least you not from China, so you no bring back the virus.' Gul and

Arsalan exchanged a puzzled look. Gul's institute back home had been circulating weekly updates about the coronavirus epidemic in Wuhan and the precautions they would be taking. Still, it was odd to hear about it from a taxi driver in New York.

The taxi dropped them off on Washington Street in Dumbo, a tiny neighbourhood in Brooklyn where late one night, his heart beating like a trapped bird, Arsalan had proposed to Gul. As they alighted from the taxi, the massive blue pillars of Manhattan Bridge suddenly came into view, as if in a scene from a sci-fi movie, and their pulses quickened. They stood for a moment, transfixed by its magnificence. They were subletting a loft for two months from Dr Karen Olsen, one of Arsalan's professors at Columbia. It was a cavernous and comfortable space—thirteen-foot high ceilings, wooden beams, furnished in Gothic style—in complete contrast to home and just what they needed. And the bedroom, with its massive four-poster, wrought-iron bed, black velvet curtains, and framed Robert Mapplethorpe prints on the walls, made their hearts race.

There was a note stuck inside the front door:

Welcome to NYC, Arsalan, and Gul! Make yourselves at home. There's basic stuff in the pantry. You can open any of the wines on the top two shelves. Emergency numbers on the fridge. A lot of concern about the virus before I left. Be careful. Let's talk on the phone.

Karen

They showered and made love. Alone together for the first time since they got married made them uninhibited and drunk with passion. Ravenous, they woke up at 4 a.m., jet lagged. Arsalan made eggs and toast, slathered with butter. Gul, usually dressed modestly in the house they shared with

Abbu Jaan and Ummu Jaan, Arsalan's father and mother, walked around the loft naked, randomly picking out titles from Dr Olsen's bookshelves: *Punks, Poets, Provocateurs*; *Art of the Middle East*; *Araki by Araki*; Céline's *Death on the Installment Plan*; Camus' *The Plague*. Arsalan lay wrapped in a blanket on the black velvet couch, watching Gul's body curve diaphanously in the early morning light from the French windows.

She brought the books to him. They leafed through Araki's bondage photography of Japanese women in silk kimonos, suspended from ceilings, their legs spread apart, hairy vaginas and small breasts exposed, tied up in velvet ropes. 'Let's fuck,' Gul commanded. They made love again, this time savagely, hungry for the forbidden pleasures they couldn't indulge in back home. No one heard their raucous ravaging of each other; no one heard their wild release. The Q train thundered across the Manhattan Bridge while the clementine sun rose above the East River.

II

At Columbia, Zeyneb Kaya, an environmental activist, and filmmaker—all waist-length black hair and a pierced nose—had been obsessively in love with Arsalan. Until she decided she was a lesbian and left him for Zoey, a gorgeous, blue-eyed blonde from Iowa whom she met at an Extinction Rebellion rally. They got married and moved to Bushwick where they ran a vegan restaurant with a back room that screened progressive films from female directors. She was excited to see Arsalan again and meet his wife, Gul, for the first time. Zeyneb had read about Gul's fierce fight for women's rights in her country and often seen her in photographs, as an advocate for the underprivileged—

the defiant, modern face of the Middle Eastern woman. They arranged to meet at Cecconi's restaurant by the river. Zoey, four months pregnant with their first child, was a bit nervous and had stayed home. Fear and uncertainty were all around. People they both knew had fallen sick. Some were in hospital. Zoey's aunt in Queens had died. Just turning on the news brought a creeping sense of impending doom.

And yet, while waiting for Arsalan and Gul to show up, at a table at Cecconi's overlooking the river, it occurred to Zeyneb that you couldn't tell there was a pandemic lurking in the shadows of the city. The restaurant was nearly full and vibrating with energy. There was laughter, glasses clinking, attractive people huddling over food and wine, and then suddenly floating through the fragrant haze, Arsalan and Gul appeared like movie stars and enveloped her in warm hugs.

They talked, ate, and drank for hours. Gul was bewitching. Zeyneb felt giddy in her company. And Arsalan had grown a beard and matured into a sagacious chronicler of the times. In conversation, he reminded her of Orhan Pamuk, the celebrated Turkish writer. Eventually, they spoke about the virus. Zeyneb was surprised how little the visitors knew about the pandemic situation in the USA, especially in New York. She told them there were already 1,000 confirmed cases of Covid-19 in the city, and more than ten people had died. The city was going to be shutting down in a few days.

After dinner, they walked down to Jane's Carousel. The exquisitely restored merry-go-round in its translucent glass enclosure was empty of children at this hour, its horses, lost and forlorn, waiting for no one. They were all a little drunk. 'America is spinning out of control,' Zeyneb said, and lit a cigarette, looking across the river at the silver shadows of the skyscrapers of Manhattan, punctured by lights. She turned to face them, a gypsy princess with kohl-lined eyes and scarlet lips, in a glistening black dress and fake-fur coat. Behind her, the illuminated span of Brooklyn Bridge looked like an enormous bird, its wings spread out, about to take flight. 'We're pretty fucked, you know. This America is not the place we dreamed of growing up far away, listening to Pearl Jam on MTV. And it's not Obama's America we came to study in; those seem like the golden years now.' Arsalan remembered that time vividly. Obama was the first US president to mention their country on TV in a UN speech. It had given him and Gul a thrill. And America may still have been an arrogant, imperialistic, fucked-up nation, but under Obama's watch, it was the closest it came to its ideals.

Zeyneb took another drag. She had been restless and angry even before the pandemic arrived. So many Americans didn't understand the urgency of the situation. 'A madman is in the White House; white supremacists are hunting down innocent black men. Thousands are starving in this most prosperous, fucking country in the world. Republicans are raping the environment. Zoey has so much debt from college; we'll probably be paying it off until we are old! And now this virus. Have you switched on the TV yet? Have you heard them talk about it—they have no clue what to do! It's like we're living in a third-world country. We have no idea how to handle it.'

It was beginning to get cold. Gul shivered in her jeans and leather jacket. With a pang of guilt, she wondered if they had made the right decision to come to New York. She had looked at all the WHO reports, read the news every day, which said it would be safe for them to travel. Arsalan put his arms around her from behind, guessing her thoughts. Zeyneb flicked her cigarette into the river. In the amber light from the carousel, Gul looked cinematic in Arsalan's arms. Her earrings glowing like tiny moons, she reminded Zeyneb of the lovely, lost girls of her youth, in cafés of Cihangir in Istanbul. Suddenly a powerful sense of nostalgia and sadness overtook her. She walked up to them and took Gul's face in both her hands, and looked into her eyes. 'You are so beautiful,' she said in Turkish, forgetting for a moment her friends didn't know the language. Tiny black streams of eyeliner trickled down her cheeks. She kissed Gul on the mouth like a lover, 'I hope I see you again, jaanam,' she said and walked away.

III

Meeting Zeyneb had shaken them. Weirdly, it was unsettling and comforting, both at the same time. They began to get concerned about the pandemic. The news was pretty grim and getting worse every day. Should they return home? There were no flights out of the city. There had been many deaths in the Seattle area. The governor of New York was going to announce a shutdown for the state in a few days. They decided to walk across the Brooklyn Bridge to the city while they could. It was a perfect spring day, and the contrails of jets from LaGuardia airport streaked the cloudless blue sky. Lower Manhattan was bustling with bankers, hustlers, lovers, saints, and cantankerous shopkeepers. It's what they had missed all these years: the electricity leaping off Chinatown sidewalks as tourists bought fake Rolexes, the trumpeter on the corner of Lafayette and Canal blowing his heart out to no one in particular. People spoke a dozen tongues, taxi drivers cursed pedestrians. Arsalan and Gul both wore the masks and gloves they had packed as a precaution. They noticed only the Asian tourists had these on.

Arsalan wanted to visit The Strand bookshop, so they strolled up Broadway, all the way up to Union Square. The city was saturated in Kodachrome light, a set for every outsider's dream of American utopia. At Wholefoods next door, anticipating a few weeks of lockdown, they bought some pasta, juices, rice, beans, vegetables, fruits. There was a joke in the family that Arsalan could not cook anything except eggs. 'Perhaps I can learn to expand my repertoire as a chef while we are here,' he said as they wandered the aisles. Gul laughed. 'You made fried eggs on toast the other night; I can teach you how to make an omelette.' Impressed by the vast array of spices available in the store, she decided to get some for the classic mountain dishes her mother had taught her. Arsalan loved them.

IV

A week passed. A sense of panic and dread overtook the city. Gul and Arsalan watched the strange and terrible spectacle of the pandemic unfold on American media. They were stunned to see mayors and doctors from various states pleading to the federal government for help. Governors were beseeching the president for increased testing capabilities, emergency equipment, ventilators, and even essential medical supplies like masks, and gowns on national TV. Supermarkets had run out of basic supplies like disinfectant and hand sanitiser. People started hoarding toilet paper, soap, and pasta; fights were breaking out in grocery store aisles. With shelter-in-place orders, they barely left the apartment, dumbfounded spectators to a sad circus while the head of state of the greatest country in the world seemed intent on destroying it from within.

They spoke with Gul's mother, then Arsalan's parents, who were panicking about their children being in the epicentre of the disease. Suddenly from afar, America the Great had been downgraded to a place of rampant infection as if it were sub-Saharan Africa. Relatively, their own country seemed to be doing fine: the king had shut down the nation for eight weeks, all government workers were paid their full salaries, and private businesses were instructed to do the same. The government was even delivering food to the elderly. There were less than 600 infections reported; only three people had died so far, and hospitals were preparing for a broader outbreak.

Gul and Arsalan had not anticipated spending their belated honeymoon in an industrial Brooklyn loft in forced quarantine. They made the most of it for the first week, relishing each other's company, watching obscure films on Netflix, listening to music, dancing naked, and arguing about politics. To distract themselves from the horrific images on TV, they made lists of things they would do in New York as soon as it reopened, breaking the previous day's record of how many times they could make love in a day.

It was March 31st, Arsalan's birthday; he had just turned thirty-eight and felt a palpable sense of history in his bones. That evening, Gul cooked him an extravagant meal of wild rice pilaf with morels and cremini mushrooms, a stew of tomatoes, potatoes, and eggs, and a pear and goat cheese salad. For dessert, a week ago she had ordered a chocolate cake from Almondine, a little French bakery in the neighbourhood, and they kept their word.

Arsalan watched his beautiful wife from across the kitchen counter, in a translucent black dress and antique

Persian earrings. Her mouth was painted the colour of blood, she was cooking a meal for him with tender devotion, and he felt a powerful rush of love. He arranged the ingredients she was using artistically on the granite kitchen countertop and decided to film Gul preparing the rice and stew from her mother's recipes. One day soon, he would surprise her by cooking the same dishes, perhaps even adding a unique twist.

Soon the aroma of Middle Eastern spices gently swirled in basmati rice and filled the loft. Notes of saffron and cinnamon, cardamom and cilantro floated above the arrangement of peonies and lilies on the dining table. Opening a bottle of Châteauneuf du Pape, a birthday gift from Dr Olsen, they felt heady as if marooned on a magical island of beauty and pleasure.

After dinner, they took a walk down to the park. It was cold. The cobblestone streets were deserted and seemed forged out of metal under the watery moonlight. Old warehouses appeared to be made of charcoal as if in a panel in a superhero comic book. The Empire State Building, framed between the pillars of the Manhattan Bridge, flashed with rotating red lights in honour of the city's emergency workers. The river flowed molten silver in slow motion. They stood silently, watching the Brooklyn Bridge for a while, feeling like the only lovers left alive in all of New York City. Gul put her arms around Arsalan and held him tight. 'Happy birthday, my love,' she said. He felt a million stars suddenly descend from the sky and hang within arm's reach.

They pleasured each other ferociously that night, reaching into places of magic and mystery they had never been, spitting out words of lust and longing they had never admitted to each other. They fell asleep and woke and made love again. Around dawn, Gul's naked body felt feverish in Arsalan's arms. He had her put on a t-shirt and drink a glass of water. 'Hey, darling, are you all right?' he asked. 'Yeah, just exhausted,' she murmured and closed her eyes.

Arsalan rose, made coffee, and cleaned up. After an hour, he put his hand on Gul's forehead. She was burning up. He called Dr Olsen. *Is there a thermometer in the house?* Dr Olsen told him there was also Tylenol and other medication, that it was probably just the 'flu. But Gul had a fever of 103°C and said her body was aching as if she had run ten miles. Arsalan made her tea and held her in his arms. When she was able to get out of bed to brush her teeth, Arsalan asked if she had any other symptoms. 'I have the coronavirus, darling, I am quite sure,' she said, calmly, 'The only question is how we are going to manage this, and if you have it too.'

Gul's fever elevated, and by evening, it was 105°C. The Tylenol wasn't helping. They had been following the news: 70,000 infections reported in New York City, with more than 2,500 deaths. Hospitals had exceeded capacity, and there was an acute shortage of supplies and medical staff. No one in the country seemed to be in charge of managing the pandemic. They knew it would be impossible to get tested for coronavirus or admitted to the hospital without life-threatening symptoms. She called her mother and consulted with some of her medical colleagues back home. There was nothing more to do but hope the symptoms didn't get worse. Arsalan called his parents and Zeyneb. At dawn, Gul's body was still aflame. Her face was pallid, and she was sweating when she woke abruptly and asked Arsalan to open the bedroom windows. 'I can't breathe, baby.' He called 911.

Light blue rain fell on trees as the ambulance tore through the streets of Brooklyn. Arsalan sat next to the paramedic and held Gul's hand as she lay on the stretcher with an oxygen mask on her face. A doctor interviewed him outside the Brooklyn Hospital Center Emergency entrance. *Where had they travelled before arriving in New York? What were her symptoms? What about his symptoms?* He helped them wheel Gul out of the ambulance. As he kissed her forehead, his lips felt her heat. 'You're going to be fine, baby, I'll be with you.' Handing the small bag he had packed for her to the paramedic, they took her away. Arsalan was given a swab test, handed a mask and surgical gloves, and asked to wait inside a tent along with many other people.

Dozens of doctors, nurses, medical staff, volunteers, and relatives, some with makeshift masks, were milling about. Arsalan saw the actor, Alec Baldwin, sitting in a red plastic chair. He wasn't wearing a mask or gloves and was leaning back; his eyes closed as if resting after delivering a monologue. There were announcements on loudspeakers asking people to clear the area, maintain social distancing, wear masks, use hand sanitiser, not crowd the passage to the emergency entrance. A staccato burst of police sirens pierced the gloom every few minutes as if a giant had stomped on a litter of puppies. The place had a tattered, tragic look about it—a war zone with the vanquished side counting its losses. A woman was kneeling on the ground with her head in her hands, sobbing loudly. Arsalan saw a long, refrigerated truck slowly backing into the street across the road from the tent he was sitting in. Gurneys loaded with corpses in body bags were being wheeled out of a side entrance of the hospital and volunteers pushed the bodies up the ramp into the truck. Arsalan felt bleak and faintly nauseous watching.

A black male nurse in scrubs and a face shield entered the tent and called out Arsalan's name. He introduced himself as Richard. 'Your wife is stable for now, but she will need to be in ICU for a while,' Richard said. 'We don't have your results yet, and cannot admit you without acute symptoms, so we suggest you go home and self-quarantine.' Richard went over a list of phone numbers to call, and protocols to follow in case he developed shortness of breath or high fever. The hospital would call once his coronavirus results were available. No, he could not see his wife; the ICU was strictly off-limits for all visitors. 'Here are the two critical numbers you need to know,' Richard said. 'Janine is the nurse taking care of your wife, she will provide updates morning and evening, and maybe facilitate FaceTime calls when possible,' Richard flipped his chart to make sure he covered everything. 'Dr Kushnick is in charge. He will call only with important news, good or bad. As you can imagine, he is overworked, so if he calls, please make sure you respond,' Richard said and handed over a stack of forms to sign. 'And finally, I would assume you have the virus too, so, please maintain quarantine rules.' The rain had stopped. Arsalan took the new mask and gloves Richard gave him, punched the Dumbo address into Google Maps, and started the lonely walk back to the apartment without Gul.

V

Dr Olsen's apartment, redolent and enticing with Gul, was desolate and foreboding without her. Richard left a message to confirm that Arsalan had tested positive for Covid-19. He repeated his earlier instructions. Janine, a thoughtful sounding graduate of NYU Meyers College of Nursing, called every morning to provide an update on Gul's condition. Her oxygen levels were hovering around 94 per cent. On FaceTime, his wife looked fragile, and suddenly a stranger, surrounded by tubes and apparatus, with ghostly blue shadows of medical staff moving around her, but she managed to wave. Arsalan's parents and Gul's mother called on WhatsApp morning and evening; their anxiety made him feel even more helpless. Friends and relatives left messages of shock and consolation. Everyone was praying for them to survive this terrible scourge. Zeyneb and Zoey delivered food from their restaurant to the loft.

Arsalan no longer noticed if it was day or night outside. Sitting mindlessly in front of the television most of the day, he snapped out of the neon haze only to take phone calls. He was in a fog of dread. In a span of a few days, his life seemed to have disintegrated. His wife was seriously ill in a foreign country with a mysterious disease, and he could not save her. America itself was unravelling, its president unhinged, its vast and powerful machinery dysfunctional, unable to protect its citizens from dying by the tens of thousands. He flicked on the TV. It was April 5th and the governor was warning people to expect the worst week in terms of the number of deaths; 4,600 people had died in New York alone. Another thousand would die today. 'Many folks we know and love will be gone soon,' an epidemiologist from Princeton commented, matter-of-factly. There was an acute shortage of hospital beds, testing kits, and specially ventilators. With so many deaths, the city had run out of space in morgues and cemeteries. The mayor was said to be considering public parks as temporary places of burial. Funerals were taking place on FaceTime.

Arsalan had no symptoms yet, but he had lost his appetite. Drinking wine throughout the day, he read the news in a hopeless, soporific limbo. The president was contradicting medical experts, blaming China, promoting disinfectant and UV light as a cure, accusing the WHO, boasting about the ratings of his daily press briefings, and attacking female reporters questioning his lack of leadership. A news anchor, his face etched with pain and disbelief, was reporting on millions of people suddenly unemployed, the president's grotesque handling of the situation, his contempt for loss of life, the lack of preparedness, delays, and mismanagement, and the national and global devastation that would follow. The next segment began with a clip of the president's son-in-law, a smirk on his face, talking about how successfully the pandemic was being managed.

Surreal back-to-back scenes of tragedy, wilful ignorance, everyday heroism by doctors and frontline workers, corruption, and opportunism played out on the screen. Arsalan wondered if the virus had begun corroding his lungs and his brain when the phone lit up with Dr Kushnick's name. 'I don't have good news, I am afraid,' the doctor said. Arsalan's heart began thumping loudly. 'Your wife's oxygen levels have dropped to 89 per cent on six litres of oxygen since last night. I hope it doesn't fall further. We're trying to keep her above 85 per cent, so she doesn't need a ventilator. There are none free at the moment. We are trying our best.' The word 'ventilator' stabbed Arsalan in the chest. 'The next few days are critical for her; I will call you again if there is an update. Hang in there.'

Arsalan was overcome with desolation and haunted by thoughts of Gul dying loveless and alone in the ICU, needles in her veins, and plugged into machines. Her final moments green blips on a screen. He felt a storm of rage building inside, and his head began pounding. He found Tylenol in

Dr Olsen's medicine cabinet and a bottle of Clonazepam next to it. The label showed an expiration date of August 23rd, 2018. He swallowed three pills.

'Can you try to cook something?' Gul was struggling to breathe but had insisted on speaking to him. 'You said you would learn…' Arsalan said he had plenty to eat. He told her everyone back home was praying for her, and she would get better soon. And yes, of course, he would learn to cook. 'I love you, my darling, soon you will be out of there,' he said, hoping she believed him. Janine called again a few minutes later. Gul is a fighter, she told him. Such a strong, wonderful woman and a great doctor, she had found out. 'We are all trying to get her to pull through this, but her lungs appear severely affected.' Janine sounded distraught. 'She's 86 per cent right now.'

Arsalan wanted to cry, but the tears would not come. He did not know who to call or what to do. He poured a glass of wine and looked at messages on his iPhone. He scrolled through pictures of Gul from his birthday. He missed her voice, the smell of her skin with yesterday's perfume when she awakened, his mouth on her nipples, her laughter in his ears. He came to the video of her cooking dinner. He was going to make the wild mushroom pilaf and the tomato stew with potatoes and eggs. He began assembling ingredients. Washing, chopping, slicing, dicing. Why did she, the love of his life, fall sick, and not he? He placed the phone against the bottle of wine. She was laughing in the clip when he asked her to repeat a step. 'Cut a small piece of muslin cloth—it's right here in the pantry, add two cinnamon sticks, five cloves, seeds from four cardamoms, seeds from three big black peppers split open, two bay leaves, three cloves of garlic smashed; smash them like this… with the blade of the knife...; a little bit of ginger, and yes...I have to add a little bit of birthday love...' and she had leaned over and kissed him. Then she tied the cloth with the spices into a little pouch to be added to the rice and mushrooms.

The Clonazepam and pinot noir made Arsalan's head swirl. He stopped the video and played it back again. Fucking America. The richest country in the world. Home of the brave, land of the free! Walking back from the hospital, he had seen a nurse taking a cigarette break, wearing what looked like a black garbage bag—a country of hypocrisy and illusions—of the filthy rich and the desperately poor. Forty thousand people had died in a few weeks because the most advanced nation in the world didn't have a functional healthcare system. There was no national strategy for fighting the pandemic. Where was the outrage, why was the youth not protesting? The train in his head was running off the tracks. He was gliding inside Gul; she was slippery like crushed hyacinth petals. He missed the salted honey taste of her. Where were fucking Bob Dylan and Patti Smith and Oprah Winfrey? Where were the Democrats? Why weren't the millions of decent Americans harnessing their outrage and ingenuity to ouster the monsters ravaging their country?

Onions were sautéing in the pan. *I love you, don't leave me.* 'Add cumin seeds,' she turned around on the tiny screen and laughed, took a sip of wine, and her mouth turned beetroot. He added rice, mushrooms, and water. Potatoes and eggs were boiling separately. 'My mother taught me how to blend these spices—it's a family secret,' she was giggling, a little drunk. His beautiful wife, who had saved hundreds of lives back home, was lying in a narrow bed, at the mercy of strangers less than a mile away, in a tyrannical, imperialistic, bullshit country run by a misogynist, and her husband could do nothing for her. 'Okay, just follow this closely, I won't say what I am doing.' She added turmeric, cumin, coriander, salt, pepper, fenugreek, red chilli powder, chopped cilantro, ginger, and garlic into a bowl and then she licked her fingers clean.

How fucking ironic, for them to come here to die, in the time of an ignorant, misanthropic redneck leading his blind followers off a cliff. They bombed and leached our countries, he thought, and now this man and his evil enablers, utterly contemptuous of life, are willing to sacrifice their own people for personal gain. Fuck them all. I'm chopping tomatoes, alone, stripped of my love. She is a hero for thousands. Where is the new Dr Martin Luther King? Why did we return to this shithole country for our honeymoon? Shithole country whose people will soon be the new pariahs of the world. Arsalan was hysterical with sorrow as the food cooked. He paused the video on Gul's hand, holding a glass of red wine. Black nail polish. The Cure playing in the background. The candles had burnt bright, the food almost ready. It was his birthday, but the night was incandescent with her beauty.

He cleaned the kitchen but didn't bother tasting the dishes he had just cooked. He took pictures of the rice and stew, ceremoniously presented, and texted them to Janine to share with Gul. He didn't hear back. He wished she was there to share the first dinner he had ever cooked for them. He laid the table for two. He poured himself another glass of wine.

The afternoon wore on, slowly, painfully, like a wounded horse. Arsalan lay on the couch in a stupor. He felt emptier than the street below. Suddenly the silence was broken by the clanging of pots and pans, shouts and applause for essential workers fighting the pandemic, a new ritual in New York at 7 p.m. every night. He didn't hear the phone ring or see the missed call from Dr Kushnick.

Recipe: Gucchi Pilaf
(Wild Mushroom Pilaf)

Ingredients:

110-140 gm fresh or dry morel mushrooms
1 shallot / onion
2 tbsp coconut oil
3 cups aged basmati rice
1-2 cinnamon sticks
5-6 black peppercorns
1 tsp cumin seeds
3-4 cloves
2 bay leaves
Pinch of saffron
Medium piece of ginger
4-5 garlic cloves
2 black cardamom seeds
2 green cardamom seeds
Himalayan pink salt to taste
Cheese cloth square and string
Fresh cilantro for garnishing

Method:

- Wash and soak rice for 10 to 15 minutes. Soak saffron in a little warm water.
- Wipe mushrooms with paper towel and set aside.
- Crush garlic and ginger and place in cheesecloth. Add

cinnamon, peppercorns, cloves. Fold corners of square and tie with string to make a small bag.

- Heat coconut oil in a pan. Add thinly sliced shallot, cumin seeds, bay leaves and cardamom seeds. Fry on medium heat till shallot is brown. Add morels and fry gently for 5 minutes. Add rice without water and fry for another 5 minutes. Add 5½ to 6 cups of water, saffron and salt. Lastly, add the bag of spices. Stir and cover the pan.
- After the rice starts to boil, place the pan on low heat for 5 to 10 minutes. Fluff rice with a fork and turn off heat once the rice is done. Wait for 5 minutes before serving.
- Garnish with coriander and remove bag of spices. (The cheesecloth can be washed and reused.)

Acknowledgements

The memory of being five years old, trailing my beautiful grandmother as she measured out the spices and lentils for our ageing khansaamah, our cook, stays with me. She'd break off a piece of cinnamon and give me a bit to suck. Tucking her long black hair behind her ear, her sari swirling, sweat beading on her waist…These are memories where I first learnt about the transformative power and community of food. So first, I'd like to acknowledge my grandmother, Sadiqa Saran, who is the beginning of a lot of my food memories.

Thank you to Juhi Kalra who helped read, proofread and edit some of the book; and to Aparna Jha who tried some of the recipes. Juhi has sadly passed away while this book was taking shape; her memory will live on via her essay and keep touching more people. Thank you to my amazing agent Preeti Gill who took this book aboard when the whole world was shutting down in corona times.

Thank you to my parents, to my children and all the friends and family who have given me so much joy as they relished my food, graced my table, and flitted through my kitchen.

Thank you to the ghosts of ancestors past who influence my taste buds, the humming in my veins, the searching for new recipes and new stories. And to all of you, people broken and whole, who may find community in these stories and recipes, welcome to our table. Eat with us.

About the Contributors

Devika Menon lives in New Delhi and runs a baking business called Phool Kumari Bakes, a women-owned and women-led business. When not baking, she is a gender and development consultant and does freelance assignments for non-profits.

Divya Kandwal is an amateur baker and an aspiring gardener. She believes all of life's answers can be found within the pages of books. A cat lady without a cat, she cares deeply about issues of gender, race and social justice. She loves long walks, dark overcast skies, and Nina Simone. She maintains that a flower growing through a crack in the pavement is one of the bravest things she has ever seen.

Georgina Marie Guardado is the Poet Laureate of Lake County, California for 2020-2024, and a Poets Laureate Fellow with the Academy of American Poets. She is the literary editor for *The Bloom*, a contributing writer for Antioch University's *Common Thread News*, president of the Mendocino Coast Writers' Conference, and Literacy Program Coordinator for the Lake County Library. As part of the Broken Nose Collective, an annual chapbook exchange, she created her first poetry chapbook, *Finding the Roots of Water*, in 2018 and her second chapbook, *Tree Speak*, in 2019. Her work has appeared in *The Bloom, Noyo Review, poets.org, Humble Pie Magazine, Gulf Coast Journal*, and other publications. She lives with her rescue dogs Kenya and Micco, and is currently working on a full-length poetry manuscript.

Giles Duley was a successful fashion and music photographer for ten years. However, having become disillusioned with celebrity culture, he abandoned photography and left London to work as a full-time carer. It was in this role that he rediscovered his craft and its power to tell the stories of those without a voice. In 2000, he returned to photography to document the work of NGOs and the stories of those affected by conflict. In 2011, Duley lost both legs and his left arm after stepping on an Improvised Explosive Device (IED) in Afghanistan whilst photographing those caught up in the conflict. He was told he would never walk again and that his career was over. However, he returned to work and documented stories in Lebanon and Jordan, and went back to Afghanistan in 2012 to complete his original assignment. His return was the feature of the award-winning documentary, *Walking Wounded: Return to the Frontline.* His work has since been featured in numerous papers and magazines, and he has talked about his experiences on television, radio and at events.

Jaya Vaishya is a doting mother of two and a supportive wife. After being a homemaker for years, Jaya stood in for her family when times were hard. Having had no cooking experience before her marriage she learnt everything from her in-laws. She educated herself by doing a three-month certified bakery course from Kohinoor Catering College, Mumbai. She now runs her own tiffin service, catering to her neighbourhood, which helps supplement her family's income.

Jonaki Ray was educated in India (Indian Institute of Technology, Kanpur) and the USA (University of Illinois Urbana-Champaign). After a short stint as a software engineer, she decided to return to her first love, writing. She is a Pushcart and Forward Prize for Best Single Poem nominee. Her work has been published in *Poetry Wales, The Rumpus, Southword Journal, Cha, So to Speak Journal, Lunch Ticket, Indian Literature,* and elsewhere. Her poetry collection, *Firefly Memories* (Copper Coin) and chapbook, *Lessons in Bending* (Sundress Publications) were published recently. She tweets at @Jona_writes.

Juhi Kalra (JkMansi) was born in India, attending schools in Delhi and Washington, DC. She received her Bachelor's degree in British Literature from Delhi University and wrote poetry for fifty years. Her work was regularly published in online publications. Juhi was a survivor of childhood sexual trauma and spoke publicly about children's rights, domestic abuse, and mental health. She was a vociferous ally and advocate for the LGBTQ community and for trauma survivors everywhere. Sadly Juhi passed away while this book was getting published, but her work will live on through her writings.

Kashiana Singh is a management professional by job classification and a work practitioner by personal preference. She uses her fascination for writing and teaching as life hacks to find the hidden moments of worship in daily tasks, chores, and duties. Her latest poetry collection, *Woman by the Door*, is a full-length collection published by Apprentice House Press. She now lives in North Carolina and bridges the miles between the US and India by finding poetry in places and people.

Kathakoli Dasgupta, a former media and communications professional, started her UK-based food catering business, Katha's Indian Eats and Treats, in 2019. She pours her heart and soul into everything she cooks. True to her name, she loves to tell a story and hopes that her food speaks to everyone who eats it.

Kriti Dheer holds a B.A. in sociology and M.A. in social work. Her professional trajectory has led her to work as a freelance film associate producer/assistant director. More of a listener than a talker, her morning and evening cup of tea are a vital energy source! Besides cooking (and eating!), she immensely enjoys music, dancing, reading, travelling and art. Currently she is busy being kept on her toes by her two-year-old and resides in New Delhi.

Lina Krishnan is a writer and abstract artist. *Small Places, Open Spaces*, is her chapbook of nature verse. Her poems, essays, and paintings have been featured in magazines such as *Shot Glass Journal* and *Himal Southasian*, and have also been included in several anthologies, among them, in the *Yearbook of Indian Poetry in English*, Volumes 1 and 2. Lina lives in Auroville, an avant-garde township on the southern coast of India.

Manjari Agarwala is a natural shapeshifter. Currently, she teaches yoga to individuals and small groups with therapeutic needs. She facilitates Action Learning—a process for individual and organisational development—at School for Social Entrepreneurs in Delhi, and is endlessly inspired by it. Organising healing forest walks to reconnect urban populations with nature is another regular activity. She thrives on laughs, dreams and stories.

Mekhala Saran is a legal journalist. Her work is situated primarily in the intersection of human rights and law. She is also a poet, an aspiring novelist, and generally quite funny, both in terms of her sense of humour and her general disposition. Her favourite person in the whole world is her nephew Shubharth. You can find her on Twitter and Instagram @mekhala_saran

Nusrat Durrani is a New York-based media executive, filmmaker, writer, and photographer. During the coronavirus pandemic, he went through a transformative experience in Brooklyn, one of the global epicentres of the virus, which he survived, but thousands of others did not. Cooking helped him through the trauma.

Paresh Tiwari writes his poems and stories sitting by the shuttered comic book stores. His first readers almost always are the mongrels of his street. A Pushcart Prize nominee, he has published three collections and co-edited two volumes of poetry. His second book, *Raindrops Chasing Raindrops* was the winner of Touchstone distinguished book awards constituted by the Haiku Foundation, USA. His latest collection, *Now a Poem, Now a Forest* is available online.

Payal Kapoor, a culinary school graduate, had to reinvent herself after becoming blind and partially deaf nearly thirty-one years back due to an irreversible medical incident. She is a diversity advocate, and a disability synergiser—a strong voice for many like herself through her writings, talks, and workshops, under her recent initiative, Sens-it-eyes. A TEDx speaker, in the hall of fame in the 'She the People 40 over 40' list, she is the only known blind person to be certified as a First Aid & CPR service provider. Payal is the creator and host of the award-winning podcast 'Rasoi Ke Rahasya', empowering the visually impaired to embrace their kitchens—safely and accessibly. When not working, Payal reads copiously, experiments in her kitchen, and travels to new destinations.

Pooja Priyamvada is a mindfulness and grief counsellor, sexual wellness coach, corporate trainer, mental health and suicide prevention activist. Currently she is academic director at International Institute of Mass Media (IIMM) Delhi and course facilitator of 'Leadership & Management in Health' offered by the University of Washington. She is the recipient of the 50 Inspiring Women 2022 award by Fox Story India and India Prime Women Icon award 2022 by Foxclues. She has translated Manav Kaul's *Rooh: A novel* to English (2023) and Joseph Murphy's *The Power of the Subconscious Mind* to *Aapke Avchetan Mann ki Shakti* (2022) published by Penguin; *A Night in the Hills*, a collection of short stories by Manav Kaul published by Westland Books (2019); and *Caregivers' Handbook for Down's Syndrome* published by Sangati Foundation (2021). Her ebooks, *Mental Health: A Primer* and *Lessons for Life from Death: Papa & I*, and translations, *Land of Ghosts: Iceland* and *JP: From Nayak to Loknayak* are available on Amazon Kindle.

Rebecca Vedavathy, an award-winning poet and academic from Hyderabad, works as assistant professor, French, at St. Mary's College, in the city. She completed her Ph.D on French Haitian-Canadian Women's Literature in 2020. She was awarded the prestigious Shastri Indo-Canadian Fellowship for Doctoral Scholars in 2017 and worked as a research intern at l'Université du Québec à Montréal. She won the Poetry with Prakriti Contest (2016). Her work has been widely published in many national and international journals of repute.

Richa Sharma-Dhamorikar is a dentist by degree and a public health researcher by profession. Her work requires her to write and read about psychosocial disability research and advocate for disability inclusive development. She also loves reading fiction, eating, dancing, cooking, writing, yoga-ing and travelling. A half-Delhi-ite and half-Malayali, Richa used to live in Pune and now has shifted to the UK with her husband.

Saima Afreen is a poet, journalist, essayist, and abstract expressionist. Her poems have appeared in Sahitya Akademi journals, *The Bellevue Literary Review*, HCE Review, among many others. She received 'Writer of the Year Award, 2016' from Nassau Community College. She has presented her poems at Prakriti Poetry Festival, University of Kent, University of Westminster, and elsewhere. She received the Villa Sarkia Writers' Residency, Finland, where she edited *Sin of Semantics*, her début poetry collection published in 2019 by Copper Coin. She was Charles Wallace Fellow in Creative Writing at the University of Kent, the UK.

Shahana Raza is an independent writer and video producer who has had the opportunity to work in television, radio as well as the print media. She has translated her grandmother, Saeeda Bano's memoir, *Off the Beaten Track: The Story of My Unconventional Life*, from Urdu to English. Bano was India's first woman radio newsreader. The book has been co-published by Zubaan Books and Penguin Random House.

Srinidhi Raghavan is a feminist who works on disability rights and gender justice, conducts training and undertakes research. Over the last twelve years, she has partnered with feminist organisations, schools and colleges across India to work with women, including those with disabilities, and educators on gender, sexuality, and rights. Srinidhi is a lover of poetry who writes to make sense of the world around her. She lives with chronic illnesses and invisible disabilities that impact how she engages with the world.

Sue Flowers is an artist and writer based in North Lancashire, UK. She manages not-for-profit arts organisation Green Close www.greenclose.org. She believes in the power of the arts to transform lives and has regularly used her lived experience as a carer to campaign for positive change. She says: I use artistic processes to explore how we respond to ever-changing realities, in the hope that my work opens up new dialogues and understanding.

Aside from fiddling with AI tools and writing techniques, **Sumayyah Malik** teaches English Language in labs and courses to university students in Islamabad. Experimenting with motherhood, currently she is teaching her little one to walk and compiling her first chapbook. Her poems have appeared in *The Feminist Wire*, *EastLit Magazine*, *The Deranged Anthology*, *The Rupture Magazine* and *Us, The News*.

Tamás Dávid-Barrett is an evolutionary behavioural scientist, whose research asks what traits allow humans to live in large and culturally complex societies. He is especially interested in the architecture of social networks, and the evolutionary origins of social network building traits. Tamás is based in Oxford, and was educated in London, Cambridge, Jerusalem, and Budapest. Before becoming an academic, he ran a research consultancy working all around the planet.

Tikuli is an internationally published poet, author, artist and blogger from Delhi whose work has appeared in several print and online literary magazines. Her debut poetry book, *Collection of Chaos* (2014) and *Wayfaring* (2017), her second book of poems, were published by Leaky Boot Press. Her third book of poems, *Duets*, written in collaboration with James Goddard, was released in 2018. She blogs at tikulicious.wordpress.com

Uttaran Das Gupta is a New Delhi-based writer and journalist. He has published a book of poems, *Visceral Metropolis* (New Delhi: Red River, 2017), and a novel, *Ritual* (New Delhi: Pan Macmillan, 2020). He was at the Sangam House writers' residency in 2016, and was awarded the Robert Bosch Foundation India-Germany Media Fellowship in 2018 and the Chevening South Asia Journalism Fellowship in 2019. He teaches journalism at O P Jindal Global University in Sonipat, Haryana. He reviews books frequently and writes a column, 'Verse Affairs', on Indian poetry for *The Wire*. Since 2017, he has written a popular column on cinema and politics, 'Frames per Second', for the Business Standard website.

ALSO IN SPEAKING TIGER

A BOOK OF LIGHT

WHEN A LOVED ONE HAS A DIFFERENT MIND

Edited by Jerry Pinto

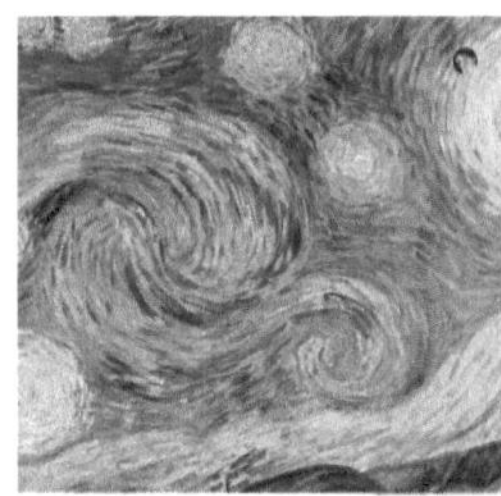

In 2012, Jerry Pinto published his debut novel, *Em and the Big Hoom*, which drew upon his experience of living with a mother who was bipolar. It touched thousands of readers, among them many who had similar experiences—of living with someone with a mental illness or infirmity. Some of these readers shared their stories with him, and agreed to share them with the world. *A Book of Light* collects these harrowing yet moving, even empowering, stories—about the terror and majesty of love; the bleakness and unexpected grace of life; the fragility and immense strength of the human mind.

ALSO IN SPEAKING TIGER IN ASSOCIATION WITH WOMEN UNLIMITED

SIDE EFFECTS OF LIVING

AN ANTHOLOGY OF VOICES ON MENTAL HEALTH

Edited by Jhilmil Breckenridge and Namarita Kathait

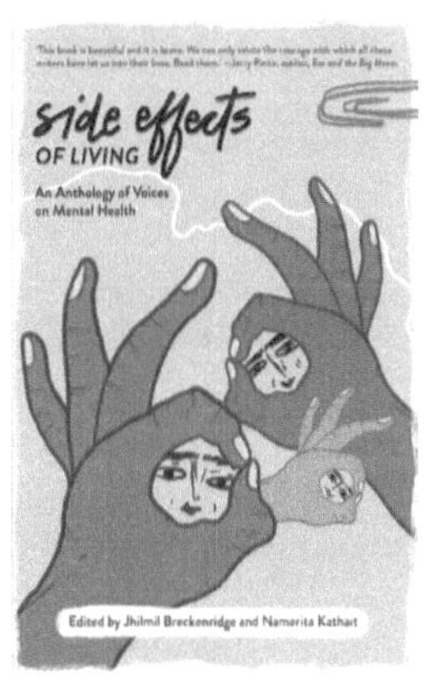

There are different sizes of bodies. There are different shades of the mind. There are different states of mind in distress. *Side Effects of Living* presents the words and verses of survivors, writers, poets and artists, who are struggling with a mental condition or have watched their loved ones suffer. Through first-person life experiences and moving poetry, they attempt to destigmatise mental health issues, as they describe what happens when the mind gives in—or gives up. Why does it happen, and can we do anything about it?

Refreshingly honest, always uplifting, this collection urges us to reject the shame and blame that often accompanies mental illness.

www.ingramcontent.com/pod-product-compliance
Lightning Source LLC
Chambersburg PA
CBHW031450160726
47994CB00005B/1961